Two Subtle Realities:
Impermanence and Emptiness

other books by
Geshe Dakpa Topgyal

Death A Natural Part of Life

*Diamond Key for Opening the Wisdom Eye:
A Guide to the Process of Meditation*

Essential Ethics

Holistic Health: A Tibetan Monk's View

The Quest to Safeguard Wholesome Family Life

Refuge

The Tibetan Buddhist Home Altar

Your Mind, Your Universe

Zuflucht — Buddhistische Zufluchtnahme

Two Subtle Realities:
Impermanence and Emptiness

Second Edition

Geshe Dakpa Topgyal

Radiant Mind Press
CHARLESTON, SOUTH CAROLINA

Second Edition, 2022

Copyright © 2012–2022 by Geshe Dakpa Topgyal

Photo credits / permissions: **Sword of Wisdom,** Sakya Monastery, Licensed under the Creative Commons Attribution-Share Alike 3.0 Unported license, https://creativecommons.org/licenses/by-sa/3.0/deed.en; **Lily Flower**, Melinda Mead Scharstein; **Manjushri**, Fred van der Zee, digitalthangka.com; **Geshe Topgyal**, Dakpa Topgyal; **Cover images**, blackdiamond67, sarinra, AdobeStock.

All rights reserved. No part of this book may be reproduced in any form or by any means, electronic or mechanical, including photography, recording, or by any information storage and retrieval system or technologies now known or later developed, without permission in writing from the publisher. For permission requests, write to the publisher at the address below.

ISBN 978-1-952518-04-1

Published by Radiant Mind Press
12 Parkwood Avenue
Charleston, South Carolina 29403
radiantmindpress@gmail.com

Author's Dedication

May the Buddha Dharma live long,
As a wholesome root for all living beings.
May the realized Noble beings live long,
To guide the confused world with wisdom light.

May everyone's wishes be fulfilled,
Whether they be worldly or spiritual.
May everyone live long with joy and happiness.
May all conflict and ill-directed actions be ceased forever.

May everyone see the oneness of humanity.
May everyone's heart be filled with love and compassion.
May everyone work for universal peace and happiness.
May everyone open his mind to the value of a moral life.

May His Holiness the Dalai Lama live long until *samsara* is emptied of suffering beings.
May the evil ideas and ruthless hearts of communist China be replaced
By love, compassion and respect for human rights and freedom.
May the conflict between Tibet and China be resolved peacefully and swiftly.

May the world not be afraid of China's monstrous economic
 and military power.
Rather, may the world be afraid of China's ignorant mistakes
 and ruthless regime.
May the people of the world come together to stop China from
 making mistakes
That are neither good for China nor good for the world.

Acknowledgment

SUBTLE IMPERMANENCE AND EMPTINESS are the two levels of the fact of reality discovered by the Lord Buddha's omniscient mind. The compassionate Buddha's spiritual scientific fact-findings about the two realities were his final and ultimate message to the suffering world during forty-five years of teachings. All of the Buddha's teachings are full of empirical observation and examination. No single word of the Buddha should be taken as true merely out of faith and reverence to him. The infallible truth of his teachings must be found within one's own personal experience by freely and openly exercising free will and using one's human brain and intelligence at its maximum peak.

I first gave teachings on impermanence and emptiness to the devoted Dharma students at the Charleston Tibetan Society in 2008–09. Afterward, it came to my mind to put these teachings into a book which may serve a wider audience. For the first edition, Jared Jones generously transcribed the entire teachings; Sheila Low-Beer and Kristin Brunson worked hard to correct the English, edit and organize it properly. For this second edition, Sheila Low-Beer has once again skillfully and devotedly worked with me to extensively edit and refine this text even further. Cynthia Laurrell formatted the book and shepherded it through the publication process.

May the merit created through their selfless work become an unfailing cause for universal peace, happiness, and harmony. May it also become a powerful cause for their spiritual attainment and may they come under the compassionate care of unerring teachers in their future lives.

Homage

My precious Guru, who is inseparable from the Buddha,
Who is the ultimate guide to all perfection,
The root of the path and happiness,
The source of the blessings and all supreme boons,
The source of all goodness and accomplishments,
The field of accumulation of merit,
And who is the kindest of the kind,
In all time, space, and conditions:

To you I pay homage, prostrate and make offerings
from my humble heart.

Contents

Author's Introduction		1
Chapter 1	General Introduction	3

PART ONE: IMPERMANENCE

Chapter 2	Impermanence: Momentary Like Lightning	11
Chapter 3	Relying on Analysis	17
Chapter 4	Analyzing Three Levels of Subtlety	21
Chapter 5	Cause and Condition	29
Chapter 6	Understanding Impermanence	33
Chapter 7	Composed Phenomena: Link to Causes and Conditions	39
Chapter 8	Intermediate Summary	45
Chapter 9	Steps to Understanding	49
Chapter 10	Further Analysis by Means of Formal Logical Reasoning	53
Chapter 11	Syllogism as Proof Assisted by *Prasanga*	63
Chapter 12	Final Review, Meditation, and Conclusion	71

Part Two: Emptiness

Chapter 13	Introduction to the Teaching on Emptiness	83
Chapter 14	*Prajnaparamita Sutra*	95
Chapter 15	Critical Points to Understanding Emptiness	105
Chapter 16	Critical Point One: Interdependent Origination	109
Chapter 17	Critical Point Two: The Object of Negation	129
Chapter 18	Critical Point Three: Mere Detection of the Absence of the *Gagja*	145
Chapter 19	Critical Point Four: How to Posit Conventional Reality	163
Chapter 20	Critical Point Five: Merging Appearance and Emptiness	175
Chapter 21	Summary and Conclusion on the Five Critical Points	183
Chapter 22	Manjushri Practice and Meditation on Emptiness	187
Afterword		211
About the Author		213

Author's Introduction

In the 21st century, many people view religion as a trouble maker and cause for conflict and disharmony in the world. People feel uneasy about religion and make effort to stay away from it, which is unfortunate and a great mistake. Many young people especially feel uneasy about religion and avoid it, but only religious practice with its unfailing energy can provide us hope and a sense of comfort and security when we go through the difficult parts of life, especially at the time of our death when we will not and cannot find anything to be helpful except our own good accomplishments based on religious teaching and practice.

Religion is not a bomb of destruction; rather it is a tool for construction, a wholesome teaching to be kept in our heart and used for making our lives wholesome, with loving and compassionate mind, positive attitude, and non-harmful actions and deeds.

Buddhism, the Lord Buddha's teaching, is a complete path leading to the attainment of Enlightenment for the ultimate benefit of all sentient beings. It perfectly fits to our inner quest for the true peace and happiness that can occur only through training the mind and nurturing the heart. Buddhism teaches with simple means how to live day by day with joy and peace, and it also teaches with the deepest means how to liberate our mind from the clinging and grasping that form the intricate nets of irritating thoughts and emotions that ensnare us. We cannot liberate our mind simply through prayers, mantra recitations, begging a divine being's mercy, or ritualistic ceremonies. Rather, we can only liberate our mind through training to develop a powerful antidote to clinging and grasping. This powerful antidote is the thorough and deep wisdom that sees the truth of reality—the way things really are as opposed to how we ordinarily and naively perceive and believe.

Lord Buddha, a great spiritual scientist motivated by universal compassion, unveiled two levels of reality that hold true in all time, space and condition. Gaining full knowledge and experience of the two levels of reality is the only means to liberate our mind from clinging and grasping—the two chronic inner mental illnesses. The two levels of reality are impermanence and emptiness. The Buddhist view of impermanence is a view of all phenomena as dynamic and momentary in nature. This view is pretty close to the view of a dynamic, ever changing physical universe as presented by modern physics.

The view of emptiness is a view of all phenomena as devoid of any intrinsic existence from their own side. Things do not have any self-generated characteristic to make them what they are. Things and objects require a designator to name them and to assign them a function. Nothing stands on its own. Rather everything depends on a designation—a term or name—for its existence.

This book offers a clear explanation of subtle impermanence and emptiness in depth, avoiding the use of complicated philosophical terms, so a modern mind can understand the deepest meaning of what Buddha, out of his universal compassion, taught of impermanence and emptiness as his ultimate message to the confused world.

Buddha Shakyamuni's spiritual scientific findings and knowledge may be used to build a spiritual aircraft to land on the field of Enlightenment. This spiritual aircraft leaves behind every form of samsaric trash that acts as the depthless vessel for pain and suffering in every single living being.

May this book be beneficial for all readers.

Geshe Dakpa Topgyal
March 2022

Chapter One

General Introduction

How do we begin to explain subtle impermanence and emptiness? At the outset, it is important to realize that before we can gain any direct experiential or insightful knowledge of these two, we have to go through the difficult, exacting process of gaining precise intellectual understanding.

Other topics of Buddhist study and practice, such as love, compassion, renunciation, *bodhicitta*, the four noble truths or the six perfections, are not that hard for us to understand intellectually, but it is tough for us to put them into real life practice. With subtle impermanence and emptiness, on the other hand, it is extremely difficult for us in the first place to be able to gain a full conceptual or intellectual understanding. However, once we have flawless and complete intellectual understanding, then it is not that difficult for us to make the transition and have direct personal experience, meditating on them to develop deep familiarity.

Our goal is direct personal experience of subtle impermanence and emptiness. To accomplish this, we need to meditate on each of them to become thoroughly familiar, but in order to meditate, we first need to have complete, correct and precise intellectual or conceptual understanding of these two.

Therefore, we study, because without flawless conceptual understanding, it is impossible to meditate upon these two subjects. To repeat, unless we can meditate on them it is not possible to gain thorough familiarity so as to have the direct personal experience and realization that we are seeking.

As we said, without complete flawless intellectual understanding, it is impossible to meditate on subtle impermanence and emptiness. This is because, in general, in order to meditate on anything, we must know how to bring the image of that object into the eyes of our mind. Unless we can bring the full image into our mind, it is not possible to use that image as a resting place, as the object of meditation. Therefore, it is important for us to study these two subjects. Through studying and learning, we will gain a complete and correct conceptual understanding of both subtle impermanence and emptiness, and then we will be able to bring the image of them into the eyes of the mind as the objects of our meditation.

Renunciation

The ultimate purpose of studying and meditating on impermanence and emptiness is to uproot the deeply embedded seed of samsaric existence. In order to be motivated to eliminate the seed of samsaric existence we need to develop renunciation, either fabricated or natural renunciation. **Lama Tsongkhapa** in the *Lamrim Chenmo* or *Great Exposition on the Stages of the Path to Enlightenment* says:

If you cling to this life, you are not a true practitioner. A true practitioner must not have a sense of clinging or attachment to this life. The effect of practice must be aimed to reach either Nirvana or Enlightenment, or, at least, to create a karmic cause for happiness beyond this lifetime. If you have a sense of clinging to samsara, there is no way to put an end to this cycle.

Lama Tsongkhapa continues:

If you do not contemplate the suffering nature of samsara, you will never have the inner urge to get out of this cycle. If you do not realize the source or origin of the cycle, you will not know the way to get out of that existence. Therefore, one should seek the realization of renunciation.

This means that if you are attached to the world, you do not have the wish to be free from that cycle.

Correct View

After you train to develop renunciation you begin to cultivate an understanding of impermanence and emptiness through study. At the outset you have to know that there are three fundamental Buddhist views of reality that work together, and that impermanence and emptiness are the second and third of these. The first Buddhist view of reality is the view of **interdependent origination**. This is the view that all things and phenomena are interdependently arising, interrelated and interdependently connected. This view of interdependence is the foundation for the more subtle second and third views, impermanence and emptiness.

In the view of interdependent origination, there is no concept of God or another supernatural being who is inherently existent, all-knowing, omnipresent, omnipotent, unitary and creator of all.

The view of interdependent origination logically refutes even the possibility of such a creator being. In this Buddhist view of interdependent origination, there is no creator who himself is eternal, causeless and independent, or who has the supernatural power to create the entire universe instantly through his or her intention.

In the Buddhist view, all things that exist, whether physical, mental or abstract phenomena, are interdependently arisen, interconnected and interrelated. So again, because of this view of interdependent origination, there is no concept of an ultimate uncaused creator. Moreover, not only are all things interconnected and interrelated in coming into being, but they are also interconnected and interrelated in their abiding and cessation.

The second of the three Buddhist views, the view of impermanence, is the view that all conditioned, interdependently arisen things and phenomena are impermanent by their nature. That all things and phenomena are being produced by the collective work of multiple impermanent ever changing causes and conditions necessitates that things are impermanent by their very nature. An impermanent cause cannot bring about a permanent product.

The third and most subtle view, the view of emptiness or selflessness, is the view that all things and phenomena have no **inherent existence**, that nothing exists by its own power, that everything is empty of inherent existence.

These views are very important because direct experience of subtle impermanence and emptiness prevents the possibility for delusions to arise, in or under any conditions and circumstances. Delusion about the nature of reality always precedes negative actions.

If you have the correct view of reality, then you will have correct actions and behavior. If you do not have the correct view, then your actions and behavior may not be correct. When we say, "correct actions and behavior," correct mainly refers to virtuous and wholesome actions and behavior. This means, if we do not have the correct view of reality then our actions and behavior cannot be virtuous or wholesome in or by their own nature. However, if we do have the correct view of reality, then our behavior will inevitably be virtuous or wholesome by nature, without need of any external reference. Correct view functions to create virtuous actions and behavior.

At this point it is good to know the meaning of **view**. For example, the first of the three Buddhist views, the view of interdependent origination, is the mental attitude that regards all things and phenomena as interconnected for their arising, abiding and cessation. That type of mental attitude or mental behavior is called a view.

Used in this sense, a view is not something at work on the level of your visual sense. In this case, it is the mental attitude of treating or regarding all things and phenomena as being interrelated or interconnected. This is the meaning of view. A view is not an action, such as seeing, holding, grasping, clinging, knowing, etc. Actions are different from a view.

Moreover, a view is not necessarily your personal conviction or comprehension of something. For some reason you might have the mental attitude of treating all things and phenomena as interconnected, even though you personally do not have full conviction in the law of interdependence. Once you have that mental attitude of treating all things and phenomena as interdependent, you find that this attitude is comfortable.

Now we will turn to the second and third fundamental Buddhist views of reality, our two selected topics, subtle impermanence and emptiness.

Part One: Impermanence

Chapter Two

Impermanence: Momentary Like Lightning

First, we will discuss subtle impermanence in depth and show how all things and phenomena are momentary like lightning.

In beginning to consider subtle impermanence, we need to understand that when we regard any object, we do not see the subtle change within that object, the hidden change that is continual. Our perceptions are not equipped to go deeper into the reality beyond the appearance. Of course, we might see various gross changes such as a hammer hitting a cup. However, we need to realize that there is always an undetected process of change occurring. The subtle impermanence that is the constant change within the object gradually leads to that object being obviously impermanent. If there would be no constant change within the object, if change would only come from the outside in the form of gross changes that we can see, change could be prevented.

Impermanence is called *mitagpa* in Tibetan and *anicca* in Sanskrit. *Mitagpa* denotes that something is unstable, unsteady, ever changing, momentary, and naturally subject to decay. The instability or unsteadiness of all conditioned things and phenomena is not caused by external force. All things are unstable by their nature, just because they are interdependently arisen. Each phenomenon arises from multiple causes and conditions—each of which is itself unstable and impermanent, ever changing. That very instability of phenomena is itself the meaning of *mitagpa,* or impermanence.

Instability is the essential nature of all phenomena. The essential, natural, instability of all things and phenomena is a natural, inevitable, consequence of being a product of impermanent ever changing causes and conditions, of being interdependently originated. This instability is definitely not caused or imposed upon things by secondary external causes and conditions. Rather, it is an essential feature of their own system and inseparable from their nature.

Presently, we have some idea that things are impermanent in that we know they will not last forever. However, we have a naive assumption seated in our heart that causes us to treat all things and objects as if they were able to last for some period of time, without continually going through a process of disintegration through natural change. We naively assume that they have the capability to last until they meet with outside destructive forces. This is a mistaken view of impermanence.

We regard, treat and behave toward conditioned things and phenomena as if they had some self-sustaining power to remain unchanged, as they are now, until they meet with outside destructive force. Although we vaguely acknowledge that "things do not last forever" and thus believe we have an understanding of the impermanence of all things, in actuality we do not understand the full meaning of impermanence and we do not have the correct understanding.

In fact, the idea or notion that things will not last forever is itself the mind grasping at permanence. This is because we assume that things will last—exactly as they are in the present moment—into a second moment. This mind is imagining some kind of permanence in the impermanent.

We assume things will last substantially into a second moment. Even if we can acknowledge that there is continual slow internal decay because we have learned in physics class that the atoms are continually moving, we grasp at an object and expect it to be still fulfilling its function indefinitely until changed or destroyed by outside force, as if it would have some permanence, some ability to remain exactly as it is for now.

The first thing we need to know is the precise definition of impermanence. As stated by **Acharya Dharmakirti** in the *Pramanavārtika* or *Commentary on Valid Cognition*, impermanence is, and I quote, "that which is momentary." It is also good to say, "that which is momentary, like lightning." Lightning does not have a conceivable time or duration in which to abide without fading in that very instant moment in which it was formed or produced. It does not have a conceivable time duration to abide, in which the process of its fading away has not yet begun. This is something to contemplate very deeply.

Preliminary Recitation

To get an idea of the meaning of impermanence we can recall that before every teaching we recite a text so that we may be qualified to receive the Dharma. This preliminary text contains a verse about impermanence. We recite:

> *Like a star's twinkling, like the flame of a candle, like a mirage, like a dew drop on the tip of a blade of grass, like water bubbles or foam, like a dream, like lightning—view all phenomena like that.*

Before every teaching we recite this, but is something churning in our heart? Do we take the opportunity to let something occur in our mind, so the words we recite are not just empty noise? If we really know how to contemplate on the meaning of the preliminary recitations while we are reciting them, it puts us into a state where our mind is fully qualified for the teachings, fully qualified as a vessel for what we are about to receive.

Preliminary recitation is not just a daily ritual in the Dharma Center or a Buddhist cultural tradition that serves no specific purpose or function. We may think it is simply an interesting Tibetan ritual, something cool to do before a teaching. This is not the way to think of the recitation. While we are saying the words, something should be happening in our mind and heart. When a sincere practitioner is reciting and deeply contemplating on the meaning of the preliminary recitation, tears and goose bumps pop up, which is a real indication of what is happening inside. Tears and goose bumps do not just come from empty noise. They show that the heart and mind are deeply moved by the true meaning conveyed in the preliminary recitation.

Definition of Impermanence: Momentary

So, now let us look again at this verse on impermanence:

> *Like a star's twinkling, like the flame of a candle, like a mirage, like a dew drop on the tip of a blade of grass, like water bubbles or foam, like a dream, like lightning—view all phenomena like that.*

View phenomena like lightning. As we have said, the definition of impermanence is that which is momentary, like lightning. Lightning does not have any conceivable time or duration to abide where the process of fading away has not yet started. Therefore, lightning is momentary.

Now understand, there are two types of momentary: momentariness of time, and momentariness of the continuum. We will discuss momentariness of the continuum later when we explain the three levels of subtlety in understanding impermanence.

The first type of momentary, momentariness of time, refers to the shortest possible instant moment that does not exist beyond its own formation or production. One finger snap is a conceivably short time that can be detected by our ordinary mind, and within this time period one specific conventional action—the finger snap—can be completed. However, Buddhist philosophers such as **Acharya Dharmakirti** have divided one finger snap into 364 instant moments. Compared to one of these instant moments, the time it takes to snap one's fingers is pretty long. Momentariness of time refers to this shortest possible instant moment—1/364th of a finger snap—that does not abide beyond its own formation or production.

In general, it seems that many thoughts arise simultaneously in our mind; however, this is impossible. Why does it appear this way to our mind if it is not possible? This is due to our confusion with regard to time. The time duration for thoughts arising, forming, abiding and ceasing is so almost inconceivably short that it seems as if many thoughts—five, six, or ten—occur simultaneously. However, thoughts do not occur simultaneously. For example, the thoughts of "This as white" and "This as black" cannot occur simultaneously. Similarly, the thoughts of "This as good" and "This as bad" cannot occur simultaneously. Thoughts occur serially so quickly that to our confused mind they appear to be happening at the same time. This is not the case.

It is important to know this from the beginning, as a basic fact. This is not just some kind of intellectual exercise where we are dividing a moment into 364 parts. It is very much related to our understanding of impermanence as a basis for meditation and realization, because it is the one that makes all conditioned things not to have the self-power to remain unchanged even for an instant moment, and therefore all conditioned things are inevitable to go out of existence without requiring to meet with outside force. Momentariness of time guarantees instability; it is such that things are forced to be impermanent, perpetually changing.

Anything which does not have a conceivable time duration to abide without changing and without going through disintegration is defined as impermanent. Anything that has a conceivable time duration in which to abide without changing is defined as permanent. **Dharmakirti** said:

> *Anything which has room for a moment of stasis, that I define as permanent. Anything which does not have room for a moment of stasis, that I define as impermanent.*

Right now, we ourselves do not have a correct view of impermanence. We have a mental attitude through which we treat all conditioned things as having some sort of room for a moment of stasis. This is what we believe. Therefore, right now, we do not have the correct view of impermanence, which is that all things and phenomena are momentary, like lightning. We need to find a way to understand the true nature of impermanence.

Chapter Three

Relying on Analysis

Hidden Phenomena

TO UNDERSTAND THE TRUE nature of impermanence we must rely on detailed analysis. Both impermanence and emptiness are said to be **hidden or obscured phenomena,** *lkog-gyur* in Tibetan. *Lkog-gyur* means that which is not apparent, obvious or evident to our direct sense perceptions. If there is something that cannot be seen with our eyes, heard with our ears, smelled, tasted or touched, then it is called *lkog-gyur,* or a hidden phenomenon. Impermanence is called a slightly hidden phenomenon, while emptiness is called an extremely hidden phenomenon.

Therefore, in order to perceive, understand, comprehend or ascertain impermanence and emptiness—at either the intellectual or experiential level—we have to rely on analysis. We rely on what is called valid, correct, logical inference. Unless we employ analysis through relying on conclusive reason, then impermanence and emptiness cannot be understood at all. This is why impermanence and emptiness are called hidden phenomena, and as we have said this is why correct logical inference is needed for flawless and complete intellectual understanding.

Buddha's Words on Impermanence

At the time that Buddha taught, formal logic had not yet been developed. In the *Sutrayana*, when the Buddha gave teachings on impermanence, he gave some examples or analogies. Analogies are those that help us to get a feel for the subtle meaning of what we are struggling to understand. They help reveal the subtle meaning indirectly. Remember the stanza from our preliminary recitation where all phenomena are likened to a star's twinkling, the flame of a candle, a mirage, a dew drop on the tip of a blade of grass, water bubbles or foam, a dream, lightning? Buddha gave these examples or analogies whose meaning is very evident to us, and that give us some idea about impermanence.

First, he said, "The end of birth is death. There is no escape. Death is certain." This means death is sure or definite. Buddha continued, "And the time of death is uncertain," which means, the time of death is not fixed. It could happen this moment, it could happen this evening, it could happen late tonight, or it could happen at dawn, early tomorrow morning.

> *Death is certain and the time of death is uncertain. Therefore, death is inevitable and unpreventable.*

Thus our life, like everything else, is impermanent. As we are born, it is inevitable that we will die.

If we think about it, we can see that birth and death are not two unrelated phenomena. Birth and death have the same nature, which means whatever comes into being is impermanent by nature, without need of a secondary condition or outside force to cause its death.

In the very moment something comes into being, that is the moment for it to be open to go out of existence. In the very moment something comes into being. Coming into being itself is all that is required for that to be going out of existence. In the very moment something comes into being, by its very nature as a product of impermanent and ever changing causes and conditions it is fragile and vulnerable and is bound to go out of existence. Coming into being as a product of causes and conditions is all that is required for that phenomenon to be going out of existence in that very moment.

The Buddha taught several other examples or analogies which give us some idea about impermanence, such as, "The end of meeting is parting or separation," and "Whatever is accumulated, ends with exhaustion or running out," and "Whatever is built, ends with collapse." Here, some people say, "What goes up, must come down."

These examples show that all conditioned things and phenomena are impermanent, and through them we can get a feel for the meaning of impermanence.

How Should We Study Impermanence?

However, as we have said, impermanence and emptiness are hidden phenomena that can only be initially fully understood intellectually by the use of logical analysis. So, how should we study impermanence? We should study it by analyzing our ordinary idea of impermanence and then going beyond it. Right now, we all have the idea or notion that nothing will last forever. However, we see conditioned things and phenomena as capable of remaining in stasis for a while, until they meet with outside destructive force. Unless we carefully analyze we will always see them as in some sense permanent.

Two Subtle Realities: Impermanence and Emptiness

Without doing some form of analysis, there is no way or means to confirm an object as being impermanent by nature with no need to meet with outside destructive force. Through studying and learning, we need to gain an understanding of impermanence which naturally comes into our awareness merely upon seeing conditioned things and phenomena in our day-to-day life. That is the main thing. We are trying to gain that type of understanding.

Chapter Four

Analyzing Three Levels of Subtlety

UNDERSTANDING IMPERMANENCE HAS THREE levels of subtlety. The first level is the **impermanence of the cessation of the physical continuum**, which we mentioned briefly before; the second level of subtlety is the impermanence of not abiding in the subsequent moment as in the first moment. The third level is the impermanence of not abiding from the beginning of the very first moment without undergoing change by nature like lightning. We will now look at these three levels of subtlety one by one.

Regarding the first, the impermanence of the cessation of the physical continuum, for example, when a house completely collapses, the shape, structure and design of the house are no longer there at the physical level. All that is there is what we call the remains of the house, or the ruins of the house. The actual shape and structure of the house are no longer there. So, the physical continuum of that house has ceased.

Taking another example, if a cup suddenly breaks into one hundred pieces, we would say, "These are the remains of the cup that I cherished so much." The physical continuum of something known as a cup is gone and the very functionality of that object as a cup is also gone. The shape, structure and function of the cup as something to hold liquid are no longer there. The round shape of the cup has already ceased, and there are left a hundred small pieces and fractions which we call the remains of the cup. The physical continuation of that particular object has completely ceased. That is called impermanence of the cessation of the physical continuum. This type of impermanence is readily apparent to our ordinary perceptions. We see this as impermanence and call it impermanence, and it comes to our mind as impermanence.

But consider this: Here we see the cessation of the cup as **caused by** its being dropped and broken by an **outside** force, and we do not see that the cup is fragile and vulnerable by nature. We do not see that the cup was formed from impermanent, constantly changing causes and conditions and that therefore it is itself impermanent and constantly changing in other, more subtle ways. We need to realize that all the gross changes that we do see are accompanied by the subtle changes that we do not see—that all these changes are just alike in that they are carrying out the impermanence of the phenomenon.

The second level of subtlety in understanding impermanence is the impermanence of not abiding in the subsequent moment as in the first moment. This means that something which exists in its first moment is unable to sustain itself into a second moment of existence. For example, the month of January has thirty-one days. The month of January begins to cease from the first instant moment of the first day of the month of January, rather than beginning to cease in the last moment of the last day of the month. Something beginning to cease does not mean it has ceased. Something beginning to cease means that it is now in the constant process leading toward its extinction, without having any conceivable moment or time in which it can remain static. This is so important to understand. By definition, in Buddhist teachings, impermanence means, that which is momentary, like lightning. And as we said before, every phenomenon—physical, mental or abstract—is impermanent, momentary like lightning.

This second level of subtlety in understanding impermanence is much more subtle than the first. Still, it is not the most subtle or final meaning of impermanence. The impermanence of not abiding in the subsequent moment as it was in the first moment is much more subtle than the first level, the impermanence of the physical continuum. Even so, there is room in this second level of subtlety for us to assume that there is a time, or moment, in which a brand new thing comes into being and, for a while, even a very short while, is fully capable of maintaining itself without undergoing change.

We can think or believe that in the very first instant moment of something coming into being, it somehow has the self-power or self-control to remain unchanged for a while and then, in the subsequent moment, somehow it changes. We ordinarily and naively see this change not as change within the product by its own nature but as change due to outside causes and conditions. In Buddhism these outside causes and conditions are called secondary conditions.

What do we mean by **secondary causes and conditions?** For example, if a flower gets too much heat from the sunlight, this heat from sunlight is the secondary cause for that flower to become wilted. However, no matter how much we prevent that sunlight and heat, the very nature of that fresh flower is that it is subject to decay in that first instant moment, without the need to meet with secondary causes and conditions. So, the inevitability of the flower to become wilted through some means is unpreventable or unavoidable by nature. That very inevitability of the flower to become wilted already exists as the essential nature of the flower; something is bound to happen to cause the lily to wilt, because an infinite number of things are happening all the time.

Therefore, since the inevitability of the flower to become wilted exists in its own system, the flower cannot have any conceivable time, or moment, in which it can remain static. The lily flower has its own natural fragility, so it is sure to lose its freshness. However, even with this second level of subtlety, there is still the possibility that we are unable to see that there is no moment of stasis in the flower. This leads us to the third level of subtlety, which is the impermanence of not abiding from the very first moment without undergoing change by nature. All conditioned things and phenomena do not have any conceivable time or moment for them to be static. They do not have room to have a moment of stasis. Therefore, they cannot have a conceivable time duration in which they do not go through change. They are like lightning.

Since all conditioned things constantly go through change by their own nature, you can say that all conditioned things and phenomena are in a moment or in a state of constantly being affected by change. They are either affected by time or affected by change. At the moment of coming into being a thing is affected by change but not affected by time. From the subsequent moment all things are affected by both time and change.

The third and most subtle level of impermanence is that all conditioned things and phenomena are in a constant state of being affected from the very moment—that inconceivably short 1/364th of a finger snap—that they come into existence.

Difference Between the Second and Third Levels of Subtlety

We might ask, what is the difference between the second and third levels of subtlety in understanding impermanence? In the second, the object is not able to remain exactly as it is into a subsequent moment.

In the third, the object is not able to abide beyond its actual creation without undergoing change. There is a subtle difference between the second and third levels. The second explains that an object cannot exist into a second moment in the same way as it was in the first moment. The third one says that nothing can exist unchanged beyond the instantaneous time period of its coming into being. Nothing has the capability to remain static beyond its instant moment of creation. It is impermanent like lightning!

As we said, the second definition of impermanence explains the inability of an object to sustain itself from the first moment it has come into being into the second moment. This second definition, the impermanence of not abiding in the subsequent moment as it was in the first moment, does not mean that something is able to sustain itself for a single instant or for some durational period—and then suddenly, unexpectedly fall apart. However, it might seem to imply this; or it might seem to imply that there is some findable time in which there is stasis. We are comparing one moment to the next. We think that there must be arising for a period of time, abiding for a period of time, and then ceasing.

This is not quite as subtle as we would like to be on this subject. Actually, these are not three separate events. These three things—arising, abiding and ceasing—happen simultaneously from the very cause that brought an object into existence. The cause for something to arise, the cause for that to abide, the cause for that to cease is the same cause that brought the object into existence.

For example, when you have a bow and arrow and you shoot the arrow, that arrow will fly as far as the force transmitted from the bow. This force is the cause for the arrow to go as far as it does, and it is at the same time the cause for that arrow to fall when that force is exhausted. So, the cause that brings something into existence is the cause for its own destruction. This is what is meant by saying that the cause that brings something into existence is itself the cause for it to go out of existence. Therefore, anything being impermanent does not require an outside, secondary destructive force. This is true for all conditioned things.

Things and objects come into being into a state of impermanence from the very first instant moment and do not wait to become impermanent after some period of time due solely to outside destructive force. The ever changing nature of the tomato seed is the cause of the ever changing nature of the tomato plant.

Presently, our ordinary mind sees all conditioned things and phenomena as having some kind of self-sustaining power or self-sustenance, and, only due to some secondary cause or condition, these things go through change and eventually cease to exist. Self-sustaining means **holding by its own or on its own**; self-sustenance means, **feeding on the self**. This is what we perceive or assume.

That type of understanding and seeing things is not the meaning of impermanence or momentariness. It is almost impossible or very rare for us to comprehend that nothing can exist beyond the time it takes for it to come into being, that nothing can have a single moment of stasis. To repeat, nothing—no object of the mind—can exist beyond the time it takes for it to come into being. Nothing can have even a single moment of stasis. One might construe this statement to mean that conditioned things last only for one instant moment and then go out of existence, but this is not the case. We will be explaining this in greater detail later on.

Thus far, we have discussed the three levels of subtlety in understanding impermanence. Between the three levels there are huge differences in terms of their subtleties. The difference between the first and second levels is very obvious, but to see the difference between the second and third, you must spend some time doing careful contemplation. It is not just an intellectual distinction. There is actually something that causes us to divide these last two into different levels of subtlety. You need to contemplate this.

Contemplation is a process of critical thinking that is effective in moving us beyond our ordinary presumption of impermanence.

Analyzing Three Levels of Subtlety

Unless we do this type of critical analysis, it is extremely difficult to see the subtle difference between these last two levels of impermanence.

Chapter Five

Cause and Condition

As we said before, because things are impermanent, the cause that takes something out of existence resides within the cause that brought it into existence. Therefore, the very cause that brought something into existence is its own destroyer. The mistaken view that sees the cause that brought something into existence and the cause that takes it out of existence as two separate entities is dualistic, because in reality the cause that brought something into existence is itself the cause for that object to go out of its existence.

The primary cause for things and phenomena to go out of existence already exists within the causes and conditions that brought them into existence. It is important for us to have some idea or understanding of this.

For example, sunlight is a necessary condition for the seed to germinate, yet at the same time, heat or sunlight also can act as a condition for that sprout to become wilted. This is pretty obvious to us. While it can serve as a condition for the flower to become wilted, sunlight is not the primary or sole cause for this. If it would be the sole cause, then a fresh flower could be permanently prevented from wilting by preventing its exposure to sunlight. Yet, preventing exposure to sunlight will not stop the process of wilting. There are infinite numbers of factors contributing to any one event—things are changing all the time. We tend to focus on only a few gross factors and disregard all the others.

Likewise, in the case of our own death—death is not necessarily determined by illness, or by age. If death were solely determined by illness, then it would be possible to prevent death. However, it is impossible for us to prevent something from wilting or dying by means of preventing or avoiding the secondary or contributing causes or conditions that only accelerate its process of aging and decay.

What do we mean when we say that the very cause that brought something into existence is its own destroyer? In the case of a cup, the potter who made the cup out of clay and the person who drops the cup, which breaks, are NOT causes but only conditions. The clay, itself always impermanent, of which the cup was made, is the cause of both events.

What does **cause** mean in general, or what is a cause? In Buddhist teachings on metaphysics and cosmology, such as the *Abhidharmasāmuccha* by **Asanga** and the *Abhidharmakosha* by **Vasubandhu**, you will find that a cause and a condition are two separate things. There is a full presentation on what is a cause and what is a condition. Cause is something without which a certain effect or fruit cannot occur even when the conditions are met.

For example, a mango cannot arise or occur without the mango seed, even when the conditions for it to arise are present. The cause, in this case, is the mango seed. So, even when the conditions of water, soil, fertilizer, light and heat are present, the mango fruit cannot arise if the cause—the mango seed—is missing. Condition is that which contributes to the cause for its process of growing and coming to fruition. In brief, cause means that which gives rise to an entity, such as a mango.

Conditions are those that determine the features, attributes, or characteristics of the result, such as the color, taste, texture, smell and size of the mango fruit. The cause does not have any bias to its fruit. It does not determine which will be sweet, which will be sour, which will be big, which will be small, which will be rich in color and which will be poor in color. Those attributes are primarily determined by the conditions. For instance, if sunlight shines on only one side of a particular mango, then the color, taste, texture and smell of that side will not be exactly the same as the other side, at either a gross level or a subtle level.

All Conditioned Things Change Constantly

Returning to the point that all conditioned things are in a constant state of change—this is a common way of explaining impermanence. Or, you can say, all conditioned things and phenomena are in a constant state of flux; this is just a different way of saying the same thing. The explanation found here is a little different. We are saying that,

> *All conditioned things and phenomena are like lightning, in a constant state of being affected by the change that is their essential nature.*

Can you see some subtle difference between saying on the one hand that all conditioned things and phenomena are in the nature of change and are in a constant state of being affected by the change within and saying on the other hand that all conditioned things and phenomena are in a constant state of change or flux? Between these two, can you see some subtle difference in the actual meaning of impermanence by saying it in two different ways?

Here is the most common way of explaining impermanence: All conditioned things and phenomena are in a constant state of change and therefore they are impermanent; or all conditioned things and phenomena are in constant flux, therefore they are impermanent. Have you ever found or seen this? We are saying that all conditioned things and phenomena are in the nature of change and are in a constant state of being affected by the change within; therefore, they are impermanent. The first two ways of explaining impermanence might leave room for the idea that all conditioned things and phenomena are in a constant state of change due to outside force. Although it is not explicitly stated, there can be room for that idea.

Since the process of change is built within their own system, all conditioned things are in a constant state of change without need of secondary conditions or outside force—such as too much sunlight, which contributes to or accelerates the natural process of decay that is already their essential nature. The words **affected** and **changed** are very similar in meaning. They both mean **no longer in the same state or situation**. In terms of impermanence, the state of being is no longer the same as in the smallest previous moment.

Chapter Six

Understanding Impermanence

Benefit of Understanding Impermanence

THERE IS GREAT BENEFIT to understanding impermanence. As we have said, all conditioned things and phenomena are constantly affected by the force of the change within. Since that is the case, then all conditioned things and phenomena cannot have a conceivable moment of time to be the same, unaffected by change. This is the real meaning of impermanence. If this understanding becomes our own view, then we are able to live with that attitude.

When we live with the attitude that all things and objects are impermanent by nature and can go out of their existence in any given moment beyond our control, we have real freedom from attachment and repulsion. Therefore, the realization of impermanence comes as a profound experience of freedom from fixation, clinging, grasping and attachment. We are then able to live very relaxed in the free natural flow of reality.

A sense or feeling of appreciation free from attachment is very joyful. It is important for us not to just hear this statement, but to know from our own experience that it is joyful. Becoming attached and resisting reality is always painful. Therefore, a realization of impermanence comes to us as a profound, liberating experience. We are liberated from the problems of fixation, clinging, grasping, longing, attraction and repulsion. Now, even when we feel repulsion it is because we are attached to some pleasure or satisfaction. If we see something dirty we might feel repulsion. Underlying this repulsion is our attachment to cleanliness.

Currently, we do not have a sense of freedom or relaxation in the way we live with reality, because we are constantly under the influence of fixation, clinging, grasping, longing and so forth. We cannot have that sense of freedom until we have a realization of impermanence. Therefore, we must deeply understand the three levels of impermanence.

A Product is Impermanent by Nature

When Buddha gave teachings on impermanence he said:

Whatever comes into being due to causes and conditions is by nature subject to decay with no room to have a moment of stasis.

Dharmakirti interprets Buddha's teachings on impermanence by saying:

The simple fact of being a product qualifies anything to be impermanent by nature.

Therefore, **Dharmakirti** concluded:

Whatever is a product, must necessarily be impermanent.
Whatever is permanent must necessarily not be a product.

Because of those two reasonings, one can conclude—with no doubt or hope of a third possibility—that whatever is a product must be impermanent. And since all things and phenomena are products of impermanent causes and conditions, therefore they themselves are impermanent.

Unless we get to the point where we can conclude, without any doubt, that whatever is a product must necessarily be impermanent, then seeing everything as being caused by causes and conditions—being a product—will not be the lucid evidence for that object to be impermanent. The whole purpose of studying impermanence is to get that final decisive, conclusive understanding. Only then are we able to live with the view of the impermanence of all things. Simply seeing things and phenomena as being produced is then the explicit, clear indication of that thing or phenomenon being impermanent.

On the other hand, trying constantly to apply logical analysis during every single moment of our everyday life, somehow forcing ourselves to live with that view of impermanence, is very exhausting. It is necessary to train in the view of impermanence through alternating analytical and concentrated meditation, so that in our everyday life the understanding of impermanence is triggered merely upon seeing any thing and recognizing it immediately as being a product of impermanent causes and conditions.

Dharmakirti further explains the Buddha's teachings on impermanence by saying:

All conditioned things and phenomena change, begin to disintegrate from the very instant moment that they come into existence. The reason why they begin to disintegrate from the very instant moment they come into existence is because the cause that brought them into existence itself is the cause for them to go out of existence, without need to meet with secondary outside conditions.

Because they are produced, all conditioned things and phenomena instantly begin to disintegrate through their own nature. Therefore, they have no room to have a moment of stasis. That very absence of a moment of stasis in all conditioned things and phenomena is their impermanent nature. Therefore, **Dharmakirti** said:

Anything that does not have room for a moment of stasis, that I call impermanent. Anything that does have room for a moment of stasis, that I call permanent.

This quotation is the primary source from which we derive the rest of the explanations of the Buddha's teachings on impermanence.

Once we know with certainty that all conditioned things and phenomena are impermanent by nature, then we know that death is not necessarily determined by age, illness, or any other secondary outside force. The first moment of birth guarantees the inevitable fact that death may occur at any given moment. No matter how you might explain any death, no matter how you try to determine, list, or enumerate the causes and conditions of a particular death, it is an indisputable fact that anything that is born will surely die. The fundamental cause for things to go out of existence cannot be found apart from their own fragile nature, and outside conditions are just the secondary hindrances for their continued existence.

Just as death is inevitable, it is clear, sure and certain that death can occur at any moment. Since death is not determined by outside force, sickness, and so forth, is there any reason why death cannot occur in any instant moment? Regardless of your belief that your heart is functioning properly, your brain is in good shape, and you are healthy, there are no valid reasons for you not to die at this very instant moment.

Make sure that this understanding becomes concretized, and then meditate upon the conclusion that birth is the cause for death, and death is the ultimate outcome of birth, with no escape. This is the process for making yourself familiar with impermanence regarding your own life, and you will then be able to live with that view, fully capable to respond with an understanding of how things truly are, without the fluctuating emotions of attachment and repulsion.

CHAPTER SEVEN

Composed Phenomena: Link to Causes and Conditions

ALL PHENOMENA ARE **COMPOSED PHENOMENA** and are therefore impermanent. Or another way: The reason why all things are impermanent is that they are brought into being, composed, by impermanent causes and conditions, and by nature they are themselves impermanent. Whatever comes into being due to causes and conditions is inseparably linked to all other things that are similarly produced.

Without a clear understanding of causes and conditions we may not understand why things are impermanent. If you do not understand causes and conditions, how things come into being, then you cannot see how there is a natural reason why things are impermanent, and you cannot really understand how things are impermanent. You can never understand the subtle meaning of impermanence, but see only gross factors, such as a hammer breaking a cup. We might realize that what is here today might not be here tomorrow. We know this based on experience. But we do not understand subtle impermanence, which allows us to see the natural fragility that is the nature of all composed phenomena.

As we said earlier, inevitable change within makes conditioned and composed phenomena to be impermanent. In Buddhist metaphysics, composed phenomena does not refer only to material things that are composed by billions of atoms. Composed phenomena include any material thing or object and also any immaterial thing or object. Material things are composed of atoms, and immaterial things are composed of instant moments—both are composed. Whatever is composed does not and cannot come into being independently without relying on other factors. Whatever relies on other factors has no self-power to remain unchanged. Therefore, since things are in a constant state of change, each moment is a moment for that to be going out of existence.

Each atom, in Buddhism, has a different function in terms of the actual formation of its result. Each atom has a different function, bringing its primary result either in the object's shape, color, smell, taste or texture. This is very similar to the explanation given by modern science about the inner workings of the formation of the material world. Anything and everything we consider to be a material thing or substantial object is the direct result of dynamic atomic interactions and their underlying subtle elemental force. Immaterial phenomena are also dynamic and instant, composed of instant moments. In general, the understanding of all this contributes to a deeper understanding of impermanence.

Buddhism's explanation of the actual formation of the world goes far beyond modern science's explanation. For example, when we say composed, any particular object or thing is not only composed from the various atoms and molecules, but is also linked to various other causes and conditions.

Causes and Conditions

Causes and conditions include time. Time is one of the primary conditions for anything coming into being; anything coming into being is somehow determined by time. As this is true, we cannot grow summer fruit in the middle of winter. Similarly, a particular thing comes into being occasionally, but not all the time. What determines that? Seasonal time—winter time, summer, spring, autumn time. This is because time is an instant moment when there occurs an infinite combination of the causes and conditions that are needed for anything to happen. Therefore, it is very clear that time must be considered as one of the most important of the primary conditions for anything coming into being. In this way, the Buddhist explanation for the formation of the material world goes beyond modern science's explanation.

As we have said, in Buddhist metaphysics causes and conditions are two different things. Even if all the necessary conditions exist, that alone will not help something come into being without the cause—one that directly gives rise to its result; and that result should be in concordance with the cause that it arose from. For example, moisture, fertilizer, soil, temperature and our own effort—in terms of taking care of and nurturing something—are all conditions. Even though all necessary conditions are there, if the mango seed is missing or lacking, then all these conditions cannot result in the growth of a mango tree.

We can conclude that condition means anything that contributes to the seed in its process of germination and growth. These are called conditions. So, while heat, water, fertilizer and soil all contribute to the seed in its process of germination, without the seed itself a sprout cannot occur as the direct result of those conditions. It is important to remember that cause and condition are two different things. The fundamental difference between cause and condition is that cause is absolutely essential for its effect while conditions are just contributing factors.

Confusing Cause with Conditions

In many cases, we confuse conditions with cause and cause with conditions. Because of this confusion we might accumulate all the conditions, but do not experience the desired result. This is because we have failed to create the cause. We make an effort to accumulate the conditions, thinking and believing that those are the cause, but the actual cause itself is missing. We naively believe that all the causes and conditions are there, but we get no result. Then we are confused, frustrated. We are confusing the conditions with the cause and the cause with the conditions. Therefore, whatever we try to cultivate by accumulating the necessary conditions, while the cause itself is missing, the result we intended will not arise.

For example, if we clear a plot of land to grow mango trees but do not plant any mango seeds, we will not see the intended result. Many weeds or poisonous mushrooms might grow, but we will get no mango trees as the result of all our labor to prepare the right conditions. This is simply due to the absence of the cause, not the absence of the conditions. Briefly stated, cause is primary and conditions are secondary for anything to come into being.

In the same way, we all have an innate desire to be happy and not to suffer. In our quest or pursuit of happiness, we are vigilant to make sure all the necessary conditions are present. However, if the main cause for happiness is missing, then all those conditions will not guarantee that we will experience happiness. This is why we are always living through confusion, frustration, disappointment, anger, sadness and depression.

So, in Buddhism, it is extremely important for us to know the difference between a cause and a condition when we study impermanence. We must be able to differentiate the cause from the condition and the condition from the cause, not only to understand the very nature of reality, and the natural fragility of all things, but also to be wise and effective in the cultivation of the inner causes and conditions of happiness, as well as the elimination of the inner causes and conditions for unhappiness.

Two Kinds of Cause: Internal Karmic and External Material

Going deeper, there are two kinds of cause, internal karmic cause and external material cause. So far we have been speaking of causes and conditions in general, but it is important to distinguish between internal karmic cause and external material cause.

We may believe that all the necessary causes and conditions for a desired result are present, but it is still very much possible that the actual cause is missing. So, no matter how much we believe that we have met with all the necessary causes and conditions for whatever we are trying to achieve, if the cause is missing, the results will not arise.

Even when we put consistent effort into making sure the conditions are all present and fully functional, if the intended result is still not arising, we can conclude that the actual cause is missing. If the conditions are all there but there is still no effect, the absence of this effect indicates that the cause is missing, even if we are not aware of what the missing cause is.

For example, there are some entrepreneurs who can find excellent locations to open their businesses, and despite having great concepts for those businesses and all the tools to make sure they run properly, they do not meet with success. Even though they try over and over, no matter what they do they cannot make a successful business. In Buddhism, this is an indication that the karmic cause is missing.

Therefore, Buddhism teaches that there are two levels of causes: the internal karmic cause and the external material cause. The cultivation of the internal karmic cause is more important than acquiring the material cause for whatever we are trying to achieve or accomplish. This is because once we have the karmic cause, it will facilitate acquiring the material cause through little painful effort.

Cultivating Karmic Causes for Happiness

Even if you accumulate all the conditions for happiness, you cannot attain happiness unless you have cultivated and obtained the inner karmic cause of happiness, because it is the internal cause that primarily determines the happiness that we aspire to. This cultivation of the inner causes for happiness has three parts: first, the proper cultivation of ethics; second, the proper accumulation of merit; and third, the proper practice for reducing negative states of mind and increasing positive states of mind through meditation.

These three practices must have strong roots in love and compassion. One does not need to be Buddhist or even religious to achieve happiness through these three practices.

Chapter Eight
Intermediate Summary

To sum up the main theme of this teaching on impermanence to this point: All composed things and phenomena are products and are thus impermanent by nature. Inevitable, constant change within makes things and phenomena impermanent. Change within refers to the inability of objects to remain in the subsequent moment as they are now in the present moment, and the inability of objects to remain unchanged from the first instant moment of their coming into being. When the Buddha himself gave teachings on impermanence, he said:

> *All three realms of existence are impermanent, just as lightning in the sky, which does not have any moment of stasis.*

Can we find a moment in which lightning is not fading away? No. Not only must we know how to answer no to this question, but we must know how to experience that there is no findable moment in the lightning in which or where the lightning is not fading away. It goes through the constant, continuous, unpreventable and inevitable process of change, of going out of existence through its own nature, not due to any outside force.

Likewise, we must know that there is no findable moment in all conditioned things and phenomena in which they are not going through disintegration. All conditioned things and phenomena inevitably are going through their disintegration, proceeding to non-being, in the very instant moment when they come into being because of change within. Change within refers to the object's inability or lack of power to remain unchanged in the subsequent moment. This quality is innately in its own nature, in the nature of any object and not something coming from the outside. It is impossible to find a moment where or in which conditioned things and phenomena remain unchanged, static or stagnant, because they have the natural inability to sustain themselves into a subsequent moment.

When we carefully examine this with logical analysis, we see that all conditioned things and phenomena are, in fact, always in the process of going out of existence with no self-sustainable power to hold themselves in stasis for even an instant moment. In the very instant moment that they come into being, all conditioned things and phenomena are in a process of flipping or changing into something that we cannot be sure of.

Since the very condition of things and phenomena is unpredictable, since things change at every instant moment, we always experience disappointment from the mismatch of how we expect those phenomena to be and how those phenomena really are. For example, whenever we build a relationship or connection with someone, we think of that relationship as permanent. **Permanent** means we assume that relationship will at least last longer than its own natural time duration, which is almost inconceivably short—1/364th of a finger snap.

Remember that all conditioned things and phenomena do not last longer than one instant moment of a finger snap. In the first instant moment of things, including relationships, coming into being, the process of their disintegration proceeding to their extinction has already begun, without need to meet with any outside circumstantial condition. The moment anything begins to abide it simultaneously begins to change. Its **natural time duration** is one instant moment and is too short for the ordinary mind to perceive.

In reality, any relationship we might build with someone else is—just like everything—impermanent by nature. Therefore, that relationship can change in any given moment, because there is no reliable intrinsic quality within it. Everything is subject to change in any given moment. But, **subject to change** leaves room to believe things will change after some time. Maybe it is better to say things are in a **state of natural change**, constantly shifting beyond our choice and beyond our control.

Unless we are able to live with the awareness of the subtle impermanence of all conditioned things and phenomena, we cannot live life free of confusion, disappointment, frustration, sadness and a great sense of loss. So, in Buddhism, the realization of impermanence is very much related to our pursuit of happiness. It is not a mere philosophical or intellectual exercise. It is not just simply for our own intellectual satisfaction.

Currently, it is rare for us to have an awareness of things and phenomena as being impermanent, unless we analyze and go through a focused thinking process. Things **appear** to our mind as being permanent, static or capable to remain unchanged for a period of time, until they meet with an outside destructive force. We always assent to or in that appearance, and we cling to things as though they existed in that way. When we have realized impermanence, the moment we see anything we recognize it as a composed phenomenon, as coming into being due to impermanent causes and conditions, and this naturally leads us to the doubtless conclusion that this thing or phenomenon is itself impermanent and has no justifying basis for our grasping or clinging.

Chapter Nine

Steps to Understanding

THE THREE VITAL POINTS that we have described to help understand this difficult subject of impermanence, in order to be able to gain a full realization of impermanence, are first, we must really see that all conditioned things and phenomena are brought into existence solely due to the mutual work of various impermanent, ever changing causes and conditions. Second, we must know that whatever is brought into existence due to those impermanent causes and conditions is incapable to sustain itself beyond the first instant moment of its creation. This is because all things are in the nature of continual change. Third, we must understand that the change in each moment is fully sufficient to cause anything to go out of its existence. We can say that things are their own destroyer due to the change built in their own system; they are not destroyed due to the outside force of tragedy.

Because things are brought into existence due to causes and conditions, they are caused and not causeless. Thus they have no intrinsic existence. This idea that things have no intrinsic existence anticipates the discussion on emptiness, which we will give fully in a little while.

The way things are brought into existence due to the mutual work of ever changing causes and conditions results in their natural lack of self-sustaining power to remain unchanged from the very first instant moment they come into being.

Therefore, conditioned things and phenomena have already begun the process of disintegration in the very moment they are brought into existence. They do not begin the process of disintegration after remaining static for some period of time.

The process of disintegration begins from the very first moment of a thing coming into being because change is its essential nature. The primary cause for things to go out of existence already exists within the cause that brought them into being in the first place. The primary cause for things going out of existence cannot be found as separate from the primary cause which brings them into existence in the first place.

How could this be the case? It is because the causes and conditions themselves lack self-sustaining power to remain unchanged in the subsequent moment without going through the process of change and disintegration. Remember the example of the bow and arrow. The impetus imparted to the arrow causes it both to fly and to fall.

Since the causes and conditions themselves lack the self-sustaining power to remain unchanged in the subsequent moment, they cannot produce a result which does not share this characteristic. If an impermanent cause could bring a permanent result, then results would not need to correspond to their causes, and causes would not need to correspond to their effects. If cause and effect could operate in this way, then natural causal relationships would be dysfunctional and chaotic.

When we do further analysis, we will come to the doubtless conclusion that the very nature of all conditioned things and objects is to go out of existence in any given moment or every given moment for two reasons: First, the object itself completely lacks the power to sustain itself from the first moment to the second moment, and second, because of that very lack of self-sustaining force, the object does not have any self-guarantee or self-choice not to go out of existence in the subsequent moment. Every instant moment that object goes through qualifies it to go out of existence. Therefore, the object's inability to remain in the subsequent moment as it is now, without going through the process of change and disintegration, is identified as impermanence. The realization of impermanence is completed by realizing the object's inability to remain unchanged in the subsequent moment. Everything goes through a constant process of change, like lightning.

Chapter Ten

Further Analysis by Means of Formal Logical Reasoning

Now that we have discussed impermanence at some length it is time for further analysis by means of formal logical reasoning. As we have said, impermanence is regarded as a slightly obscured phenomenon. This means it is an existing thing which is not apparent to our direct sense perception. Direct sense perception does not have access to the subtle impermanence of things and objects. Slightly obscured phenomena must be initially realized by relying on correct logical reasons. Therefore, we will now go into the formal logical reasoning proving impermanence, briefly explaining the logical syllogism, the three conclusive criteria of reason, and finally the meaning of dichotomy.

Syllogism

Syllogism is a system of reasoning used to refute wrong conceptions with regard to the fact of reality, and to generate clear and correct understanding. The logical syllogism consists of a thesis and a reason stated together in a single statement. The thesis consists of a subject and a predicate. The subject and predicate together state the thesis and the reason follows. In other words, a logical syllogism consists of **subject**, **predicate**, and **reason** lined up in a single sentence.

The unique quality of these three—subject, predicate and reason—is that they are perfectly and naturally interrelated, and this interrelationship helps to arrive at the final, correct and indisputable conclusion of the fact that cannot be mistaken. Let us build a syllogism:

A lily flower is impermanent because it is a product.

The subject here is "lily flower" and the predicate is "impermanent," while the reason is "being a product." There is the thesis "a lily flower is impermanent" followed by the reason, "because of being a product."

The Three Conclusive Criteria of Reason

A conclusive logical syllogism—such as "a lily flower is impermanent because of being a product"—must satisfy three criteria called the **three conclusive criteria of reason**. The first of these three criteria has to do with what is called the "property of the subject." The property of the subject is that the reason given in that syllogism must be present in the subject, and the subject must be pervaded by the reason with no possibility for it not to be pervaded by the reason under any circumstances. In the example of "a lily flower is impermanent because of its being a product," being produced is the essential nature of a lily flower, so the reason—being a product—is pervasive in the nature of being a lily flower. There is no other possibility. The lily flower is a product by nature and it shares this same essential nature with all other products. And, do not forget that all phenomena—not just the lily flower—are products.

The second of the three conclusive criteria of reason is that the reason given in the syllogism must also pervade to the predicate, or to state it exactly parallel to the above, the predicate must also be pervaded by the reason, and whatever the predicate may be it must necessarily fall into the reason without any possibility of not falling into it. This is called the forward pervasion. In our example, the predicate, "impermanent," is pervaded by the reason, "being a product," because all produced phenomena are by nature impermanent, and there is no impermanent phenomenon that is not produced.

The third conclusive criterion of reason is that whatever is the **opposite** of the predicate must necessarily **not** be pervaded by the reason under any condition. This is called the counter pervasion. For example, a permanent thing must necessarily *not* be produced by causes and conditions, and must *not* need to be produced by causes and conditions. An impermanent thing must necessarily be produced by causes and conditions and it must necessarily contradict a permanent thing, a thing that is not produced by causes and conditions. Permanent and impermanent are dichotomies, as we will explain soon.

The reason given in a particular correct logical syllogism is the ultimate proof for whatever is to be proven, since it is in the three modes—it is characterized by the three conclusive criteria of reason.

Dichotomy

In addition to the three conclusive criteria of reasoning, it is good to know that between the predicate and the opposite of the predicate, there must be a direct contradictory relationship, or dichotomy. This means that one must cancel the other. A directly contradictory relationship between two things must have three characteristics:

The first is that nothing can be both. Here that means that nothing can be both permanent and impermanent. Secondly, nothing can be neither. This means that a thing is either permanent or it is impermanent; it has to be either one or the other.

The third characteristic of a dichotomy is that there is no third possibility. Saying there is no third possibility is not exactly the same as saying nothing can be neither. In our naive mind, we think there might be room for a third possibility, some kind of alternative. We look for a third possibility because we are not satisfied and comfortable with the first two characteristics of the dichotomy. Unless we find something that matches our preconceived ideas, we are not satisfied. We either deny or defy, without reconsidering to find a new approach for seeking the truth of reality.

Syllogism and Sign

As we explained before, a syllogism has three parts: subject, predicate and reason. By clearly identifying the given subject, predicate and reason in that syllogism, then you can apply the three criteria of reason. Through this process you will see, first, whether or not the subject is pervaded by the reason—that is, whether or not the reason is present in the subject; second, you will see whether or not the reason is equal to the predicate, and third, whether or not the opposite of the predicate is the opposite of the reason.

Finally, based on the three conclusive criteria of reason we can come to the final conclusion, through which we can have full certainty of actually finding the true nature of reality—in this case subtle impermanence. If any of the criteria is missing then the syllogism is faulty and there is not a proof at all.

As we have said, impermanence, or *anicca* in Sanskrit, *mitagpa* in Tibetan, is a slightly hidden phenomenon. A slightly hidden phenomenon is anything that must be initially understood or realized by relying on correct, valid reasoning, and that cannot be directly perceived with our senses.

When we try to understand a slightly hidden phenomenon we look for some hint, clue or evidence of its existence. The terms hint, clue, reason, sign, mark and evidence are all, in this case, synonymous. We can infer the subtle reality that lies behind those signs. To look at an obvious example of a hidden phenomenon: The existence of smoke is a sign or evidence of the existence of fire. So we can build a logical syllogism, which is:

> Inside that distant house (where smoke is coming from the chimney) there is fire, because there is the smoke.

In this example, we are building a logical syllogism to ascertain a hidden phenomenon—fire that cannot be seen. We look for the clue or sign that is evidence for the existence of the fire; here, smoke is the reason. Fire is the predicate. The house where the smoke is coming from is the subject.

As stated above, the thesis is "Inside that distant house (where the smoke is coming from the chimney), there is fire." As we said, the reason we conclude this is "because there is the smoke."

Without going inside the house, we can confirm, ascertain, or conclude unmistakenly the existence of the fire inside the house solely based on the reason of the smoke, that smoke and fire have a natural relationship.

Unfailing Natural Relationship

The existence of smoke is a mark or sign or evidence of the existence of fire. In Sanskrit, all these terms are called *hetu* but in the texts you will most commonly see *hetu* translated as the word sign. **Sign** means that which is an obvious indicator of what is hidden. Between the one that is hidden and the obvious indicator, there must be an unfailing natural relationship. In this example of smoke, which is the reason, and fire, the predicate, there is an unfailing natural relationship.

Note that in this particular relationship fire is also the cause of the smoke. However, while there must be an unfailing natural relationship between reason and predicate in all logical syllogisms, there is not necessarily an unfailing causal relationship. For example, in the case of the lily flower syllogism—*A lily flower [subject] is impermanent [predicate] because of being a product [reason]*—the reason (being a product) is not the cause of the lily's impermanence.

Not all signs are at the same time causes. This is important to understand. While there must be an unfailing natural causal relationship between fire and smoke, there is not a causal relationship between being a product and impermanence. To repeat, even if there is no causal relationship, there is an indispensable unfailing natural relationship between reason and predicate, and there is this relationship between the subject and the predicate and the reason. All three are harmoniously lined up.

So, there has to be an unfailing natural relationship between subject, predicate and reason. If that natural relationship is not there, then the mark, sign or evidence does not obviously indicate the presence of the hidden object. If the unfailing, natural relationship is not there, then the sign—the reason—cannot generate, induce or serve as a basis for the arising of an inferential cognition of the hidden object, which is the predicate. There has to be an unfailing natural relationship between smoke and fire, as well as between impermanence and **product-ness**, just as there has to be an unfailing natural relationship between the subject-predicate-reason.

The Truth Behind the Sign

The awareness that a particular thing is the result of causes and conditions alone is not the same as the understanding of impermanence. Something coming into existence due to the mutual work of causes and conditions is only a sign of that object being impermanent by nature. In general, we only see the sign; we see and recognize something as caused, as a product, but we do not see the truth behind the sign. We do not see that anything which is a product must necessarily be impermanent just because it is a product. It has been caused or produced by impermanent ever changing causes and conditions. The truth behind that sign is impermanence—a readiness to go out of existence in any given moment.

As we have said, when the Buddha gave teachings on impermanence, he said,

All three realms of existence are impermanent, just as lightning.

As we know, lightning does not have a moment in which it is not fading away. Similarly, all conditioned things and phenomena do not have a moment where they do not undergo change.

So, how can we come to that final, doubtless and unmistaken conclusion that all conditioned things and phenomena are ready to go out of existence in any given moment? We can only arrive at this conclusion by relying on conclusive logical reasoning. We already know that our conclusive logical reasons must have three modes, or three criteria. The technical terms for these three modes in the Buddhist science of logic are **property of the subject, forward pervasion and counter pervasion.**

Review

Now let us review these, starting with the property of the subject. In every syllogism the property of the subject has two parts: The reason given in that logical syllogism must be present in the subject, and the subject given in that syllogism must necessarily be pervaded by the reason. To return to the example of smoke and fire, in general, fire is not a hidden phenomenon. Fire is a phenomenon that can be directly observed through direct sense perception. That is called an obvious phenomenon.

However, fire can be a hidden phenomenon under certain conditions. For example, you are outside, a hundred yards away from a building, and you can see smoke obviously coming through a chimney. The smoke is visible, whereas the fire itself is not visible. By relying on the smoke as the indicator, mark, sign or evidence, your awareness of the smoke serves as the basis for you to unmistakenly infer the presence of the fire. The smoke as an indicator can or will lead to the valid inferential cognition of the fire that you cannot see in that moment, in that condition, or in that circumstance.

The reason the existence of the smoke can or will help you to arrive at that final conclusion is only due to the unfailing natural relationship between fire and smoke. Therefore, between the one that is hidden, the fire, and the indicator, the smoke, there must be an unfailing, natural relationship. This is what Buddhists term either a natural **causal** relationship or a natural **identical** relationship, depending on whether or not the reason is the effect as well as the sign of the predicate—as in smoke/fire—or only the unmistakable sign of it—as in product-ness/impermanence.

The property of the subject determines the unfailing natural relationship between the sign and the subject given in the same logical syllogism. Another way to explain this is that the reason must be equal to the predicate. This means that whatever is given as the subject in the syllogism must share the unfailing natural identical relationship with the predicate and the reason. A lily flower is impermanent because of being a product. All phenomena, including lily flowers, are products of interdependent and impermanent ever changing causes and conditions; all products are impermanent; therefore, a lily flower is impermanent.

To review the second conclusive logical reason, which is the forward pervasion: Whatever reason is given in a particular syllogism—whether smoke, or being a product, for example—this reason must necessarily be pervaded by the predicate, and whatever is the predicate given in that syllogism must necessarily be pervaded by the reason given in that same syllogism.

The third conclusive logical reason, the counter pervasion, states that whatever is the non-predicate must necessarily *not* be the reason given in that syllogism.

Chapter Eleven

Syllogism as Proof Assisted by Prasanga

Now let us reconstruct the dialectical logical syllogism that we used earlier. To do so, we need three things: the subject, the predicate and the reason. The syllogism can be built in this way:

A lily flower is impermanent because of its being a product.

"Lily flower" is the subject. "Impermanent" is the predicate. "The lily flower is impermanent" is the thesis. "Because of its being a product" is the reason. Therefore, the lily flower (subject) is impermanent (predicate) because of its being a product (reason). This is the way to build a dialectical logical syllogism, or a correct, conclusive logical syllogism. In brief, whatever is a product must necessarily be impermanent. Conversely, whatever is not impermanent must necessarily not be a product. Therefore, whatever is a lily flower must be impermanent by nature just because of its being a product. Being a product is the only reason needed for its being impermanent by nature. To repeat, the essential nature of every product is impermanence.

With the help of those three criteria, we must see that there is no possibility at all for the lily flower not to be impermanent. If the lily flower has no possibility not to be impermanent, then it is ever changing. Therefore, it is in a constant state of flux. The lily flower does not have a findable moment in which it does not go through change and where it does not go through disintegration. Therefore, a lily flower is sure and definite not only to change but also to be able to go out of existence in any given moment; it has no self-power to remain static for even one instant moment. Once the sureness of the lily flower to go out of existence in any given moment becomes your experience, then you have a realization of impermanence.

Again, seeing the lily flower as being caused is not the same as seeing the impermanence of the lily flower. The awareness of the lily flower being caused is only the evidence used for one to realize impermanence.

Other Schools of Thought

Having defined impermanence as that which is momentary like lightning, and having proved by means of the logical syllogism that all things and phenomena as products of ever changing causes and conditions are therefore impermanent, we might think it is not possible to hold any other view.

However, some non-Buddhist schools of philosophy believe that something can be caused while, at the same time, having the self-power to remain as it is for a period of time—a moment, a week, a month, a year or an aeon. These schools believe that during that time, there is stasis in the physical continuum of that object. But as we know by now, these two ideas—being caused and being in stasis—are contradictory. To show this contradiction you can debate the issue.

Prasanga

In debate, the opponent's position is that a lily flower is being caused, is a product, but, at the same time, stasis exists in the physical continuum of that flower, which guarantees it will last as it is for a while. The opponent who holds this position realizes that the lily is a product while he still believes that the lily has a time of existing in stasis, that is, without changing, and that change does not occur within by nature but by outside force.

Can we directly establish a conclusive logical reason or syllogism for that opponent to see that any product must necessarily be impermanent and have no possibility of stasis, or do we first need to go through a preliminary process? In this case, we have to go through a preliminary process by means of constructing a *prasanga,* or consequence, so that the opponent can see the contradictions in his position. A consequence is an ironic logical statement that explicitly exhibits the contradiction between two assertions.

When an opponent holds a position that is fundamentally incorrect, then the challenger would disqualify the opponent's position through consequences. A consequence is a logical statement, but it is different from a syllogism. The consequence demonstrates to the opponent the inconsistency and invalidity of his position. The consequence can be needed before the syllogism if the opponent declines to give up his incorrect position. Syllogism will not work for the opponent if his mind is closed and he holds on to his own incorrect position as fundamentally true and valid.

For example, when the opponent accepts a lily flower as being produced but at the same time he believes it is static—that change is not inevitable in every moment—and that change does not occur continually within but only comes from some outside force, then the following consequence must be forced on him or her.

The consequence or *prasanga* can be built or stated as follows:

Is the lily flower not being produced (by causes and conditions) because of its being by its own nature unchanging until it meets with outside destructive force?

This consequence is basically questioning the opponent by saying, "Can you assert that the lily flower is not being produced by causes and conditions because you believe the lily is by its own nature unchanging and therefore you see it as static until it meets with outside destructive force? If this is the case, then you have to accept that something being a product—produced by interdependent, impermanent and ever changing causes and conditions—and that same thing being static or capable of stasis are not contradictory."

Through the force of the consequence you can make the other person see the fallacy in his assertion, causing him to reconsider or reexamine his position: "Ah! Yes, I believed it was being caused but, at the same time, I believed there was stasis within the physical continuum of that flower which guarantees that the flower will remain unchanged as it is in the present moment for a period of time." Through the consequence, he is able to see the inconsistencies or contradictions of his position based upon the natural law of logic, which causes him to give up his previously held assertion.

Only at this point in the debate or discussion can one build a new logical syllogism for the opponent, as a means of assisting him to realize impermanence through using the three conclusive criteria of reason. Prior to this point, no matter how you try to force him to see a fallacy in his position, based on correct logical reasoning, he will either argue that whatever is the reason must not necessarily apply to the predicate, or whatever is the opposite of the predicate must not necessarily not be the reason. He will say that being permanent does not necessarily mean that something is not produced.

Why is the *prasanga* needed? First, we use it to help the opponent overcome his doubt tending towards the non-factual. Second, it helps him to gain doubt tending towards the factual. And third, it helps him gain a correct assumption of the fact. Then at this point his assumption is correct; however, she or he does not yet have the full valid reason as the base of this assumption, but still sees some sort of stasis within the physical continuum that guarantees for that object to remain unchanged for a while.

Assumption means Pre-assumption

There are two types of pre-assumption: wrong pre-assumption and correct pre-assumption. Through the consequence or *prasanga*, we must help the opponent to have a correct assumption; he might think, "Oh, well, now, whatever is a product must necessarily be impermanent." He gets to the point where he has that correct presumption, belief or feeling that "Probably, whatever is a product is impermanent."

The opponent feels it is more logically feasible for all products to be impermanent, but that belief or feeling does not yet have the full valid reason as its basis. Because it does not have the full valid reason as its base, the opponent in the debate is still not completely convinced by the assertion that whatever is a product has no way to be anything but impermanent—momentary like lightning.

In order for the opponent to have a basis to arrive at the final conclusion, where there is no doubt, he or she must see the natural intimacy between being caused and being impermanent. Simply being caused itself makes that thing impermanent by nature. Once you see this, from then on, even if someone threatens to take your life, saying, "Unless you give up that position I will kill you!"—in your heart, even in the midst of fear, you will be very reluctant to give up that position.

So, in this case, you propose that a lily flower is not being caused because it is permanent. That is a consequence. In the beginning, the other person will say, "Leave me alone, I do not see a contradiction between being caused and being permanent—having some moment of stasis. I do not see the contradictions. Being caused is not necessarily being impermanent and being permanent is not necessarily not being caused." He might say this. He might become very agitated and defensive.

Gradually, you must lead him step-by-step, each time presenting or showing small errors or fallacies and continuing to ask, "Can you explain what you mean by being caused, being caused, being caused?" You allow him to explain, and ask him to explain repeatedly, over and over again, what it is that makes him believe that a lily flower is being caused yet at the same time is permanent. From the challenger's side, keep raising new questions, which force him to give new, additional explanations based upon his previous position.

Gradually, this kind of sincere and open discussion between the opponent and challenger will become more subtle. The more subtle the argument becomes, the more apparent it is to the opponent that she or he is contradicting his previous assertion.

The discussion in the form of question and answer is aimed to lead to fact rather than mere belief or assumption. Through the process of discussion and explanation, the opponent starts seeing the subtle fallacies in his position. Slowly, he will start seeing that permanence and impermanence are directly contradictory qualities. This means there cannot be anything which is both permanent and impermanent, there cannot be anything which is neither, and there is no third possibility. That is called a directly contradictory dichotomy. One cancels the other by nature.

Through this lengthy process of logical analysis based upon lucid evidence, we can prove or establish subtle impermanence in all conditioned things. In this case, being a product is the lucid evidence of all conditioned things being impermanent. Until we arrive at that conclusion after going through a lengthy process of logical analysis—no matter how we think or believe we have a realization of impermanence—it is just a mere correct assumption. We might have an idea or notion that all conditioned things are impermanent because we have heard that "nothing lasts forever," and that phrase is very much ingrained in our mind as a memory or a belief. It is just the correct answer without a basis. Therefore, both consequence and syllogism are extremely important.

Chapter Twelve
Final Review, Meditation, and Conclusion

Now it is time for a final review of subtle impermanence, instructions for meditation, and our conclusion. To begin we will return once more to our syllogism:

A lily flower is impermanent because of its being a product.

Lily flower is the subject. It is called the subject because it is the basis upon which something is to be proven. In this case, we are proving its impermanence, so impermanence is the predicate. The impermanence of the lily flower is hidden. It is not obvious or apparent to our perception, which means the impermanence of the lily flower is undetectable to our direct sense perception. This is why we need a reason to prove the lily flower is impermanent. The reason is—being produced or being a product.

So, the lily flower is impermanent because of being a product. As we said before, a correct logical statement like this that has a subject, predicate and reason is called a syllogism. In Sanskrit, the entire syllogism is called *hetu*. As we said above, *hetu* is also the word used for sign, mark or evidence. The subject, predicate and reason of the syllogism have concordance in their natural identical relationship and therefore together they make the *hetu* or sign of the truth of reality.

The property of the subject is, whatever is a lily must be a product. The sign or *hetu* within the syllogism is a **product** and it must be present in the subject lily. Therefore, whatever is a lily, or all lilies, must be a product. For the syllogism to be correct or valid, this statement must also be true or correct in all cases. This means there is no such thing called lily which is not produced. There is no such thing called lily which is not brought into existence due to the collective work of interdependent, impermanent causes and conditions. Therefore, whatever is a lily must be a product.

The forward pervasion is:

> *Whatever is a product must necessarily be impermanent, with no possibility for it not to be impermanent.*

Therefore, since a lily flower is a product it is impermanent by nature. The counter pervasion is:

> *Whatever is permanent must necessarily not be a product, with no possibility for it not to be a non-product.*

Which means, there is no such thing called permanent which is a product; also, there is no such thing as a product that is not impermanent. Whatever is a product must necessarily be impermanent. Whatever is permanent must necessarily not be a product. Therefore, whatever is a product must be impermanent by nature. This is called conclusive reason.

Solidifying Awareness of Impermanence

The next question is, how do you solidify your awareness of impermanence? You do this through contemplation and meditation. All one needs to do is go through the process of reexamining the natural, unfailing relationship between being a product and being impermanent. Go through this over and over until a powerful shift occurs in your perception, from which you begin to see the inevitability of things going out of existence in any given moment merely because of being a product.

When you start seeing things as inevitable to go out of existence in any given moment, then simply rest in that experience by dropping the words and descriptions that you used as a tool to unveil the naked image of impermanence. For example, drop words like impermanence and descriptions like, "Whatever is a product must necessarily be this, so and so forth." That is the way to take a valid inference and have it become a valid experience. This is the way to meditate on impermanence.

Vipassana Meditation

We understand that the realization of impermanence and emptiness comes from the lengthy process of analysis. Going through this process of analysis is very much related to *Vipassana* meditation practice. In order to do this type of practice, we must have the highly disciplined mind gained only through *Shamatha* meditation. Otherwise, the mind will jump all over with no concordance and no focus. Unfocused, random analysis leads nowhere and has no conclusion; it causes our study and analysis to be ineffective. Therefore, it is extremely important for us to have a mind that is supple, agile and disciplined. We train in *Shamatha* meditation to develop this mind.

The amount of analysis you use in the process of the mind penetrating into the fact of reality depends on the caliber of your single-pointed concentration. If your main goal is to let yourself be an observer, for example, to observe the ugliness of anger, then you must consciously and deliberately let the emotional feeling of anger arise in your mind. When you let that anger arise in your mind, you have full control over that anger. This is how you can keep the full force of the anger while at the same time allowing yourself be an observer. Once you are fully convinced of the ugliness and destructiveness of anger, from that day onward you are determined to avoid becoming angry, regardless of what may occur.

Similarly, through contemplation and analysis during *Vipassana* meditation on impermanence, you can allow the real meaning of impermanence to arise in your experience or in your mind. By using *Shamatha* meditation you can then hold that experience for prolonged periods of time. This is how you engage in the process of making your mind fully familiar with that experience or engage in the process of gaining full familiarity with impermanence.

Currently, you do not have a full familiarity with impermanence. You are used to seeing things and objects as having the capability to remain for a while without changing. You need to work or train to make the mind familiar with seeing conditioned things and objects as being momentary, like lightning, with a complete lack or absence of a conceivable time in which they can remain unchanged. This is the main purpose of meditating on impermanence.

For example, the more time you spend with someone the more familiar you are with his or her nature. By learning his or her nature, you know the best way to behave and interact with that person. Similarly, through meditating on the impermanent and empty nature of things and objects, you will know the best way to behave and interact with them.

Simply holding onto the word "impermanence" is not the meaning of meditating on impermanence. Simply thinking that all conditioned things are impermanent in that they will no longer be here one day, is also not the meaning of meditation on impermanence.

How to Meditate on Impermanence

Meditation on impermanence requires that you first sit in a meditative state, letting your mind become calm and relaxed. Then, let your mind go through a lengthy analytical process until the clear image of impermanence arises in your awareness. When that happens, let words and descriptions go, and simply rest in the experience of the inevitability that things can go out of existence in any given moment, just because of the change that occurs within them. Since change within is built into their own system, it cannot be altered or prevented by any outside, external means. **Dharmakirti** said:

> *Change within cannot be stopped through any means.*

Therefore, it is inevitable that objects can go out of existence in any given moment. Once that powerful awareness occurs, simply rest in that experience, without mulling, for an extended period of time. This very act of resting in the awareness of the lack of stasis in all conditioned things and phenomena is called meditation on impermanence.

Identical Relationship

In order to deepen understanding of the syllogism proving impermanence, it is very important for us to be thoroughly familiar with the meaning of **unfailing natural relationship** or **identical relationship**, which we have discussed briefly before. It is important to understand the identical relationship between being a product and being impermanent; these two are identical in nature. However, while being a product is obvious, or evident—we can see that all things and phenomena are the result of causes and conditions—subtle impermanence is hidden.

Since there is an unfailing natural, identical relationship between being a product and being impermanent, products cannot be anything but impermanent by nature.

Dharmakirti says it is difficult for us, in the first place, to understand that **being a product** and **being impermanent** are identical in their nature. **Identical in nature** does not mean that product-ness and impermanence are one or that they are the same thing. Usually, identical means that two or more things are exactly alike; for example, identical twins who look alike. But in this case, an identical relationship means simply that something being a product necessitates its being impermanent and something being impermanent necessitates its being a product.

A product has the nature of being impermanent, and at the same time something impermanent has the nature of being a product. This reciprocal relationship between being a product and being impermanent is what we call being identical in nature. Therefore, something being a product makes it imminent to cease at any given moment, without need of a secondary external destructive force. It is by its very own nature impermanent, like lightning.

We can contemplate this as a way to evoke the meaning of impermanence in our mind: Being a product and being impermanent are identical in their nature. Therefore, being a product is the powerful, unmistakable and conclusive sign or reason that establishes a thing as impermanent by nature.

A lily flower is impermanent because of its being a product. Unless we are able to establish and recognize something as being impermanent just because of being a product, there is no way for us to develop a clear, valid idea of impermanence in our mind. There is no other avenue or access for us to bring the clear image or meaning of impermanence to our mind. So, something being a product must inspire us to infer and to recognize it as being impermanent.

Being a product by itself must serve as the direct, or immediate, condition for us to establish a valid inferential cognition of impermanence. Without this cognition, there is no possibility for us to have a spontaneous awareness of something being impermanent simply because it is a product. Simply thinking about the word impermanence, or repeating the word "impermanence" or the words "change within" over and over in our mind, will not help us to develop a correct understanding or realization of impermanence.

When there is an identical relationship between two things, the characteristics of that identical relationship are, first, the moment one comes into being the other must also come into being. Second, the moment one ceases to exist, simultaneously the other must go out of existence in that very instant. One part goes out of existence solely because the other part went out of existence, with no other reason, even though these two are not the same thing.

Forward Pervasion, Counter Pervasion

Once you are able to see the identical relationship between being a product and being impermanent, then it is fairly easy to see something automatically as impermanent, merely upon seeing something as a product, the moment you recognize anything as a product. Being a product spontaneously confirms its being impermanent. Unless you understand that, it is not possible for you to establish the three modes of the logical syllogism. If you do not have a clear understanding of the identical relationship between product-ness and impermanence you cannot establish the forward pervasion and counter pervasion.

The forward pervasion is, "Whatever is a product must necessarily be impermanent." The counter pervasion is, "Whatever is permanent must necessarily not be a product." It is impossible for something to be both permanent and a product. It is also impossible for something to be a product but not be impermanent. Therefore, whatever is a product must necessarily be impermanent by nature, and whatever is not impermanent must necessarily not be a product.

Since a lily flower is a product, it must be impermanent, without room for further questions, doubt or hesitation, with no possibility for it not to be impermanent. When you arrive at that final conclusion that whatever is a product must necessarily be impermanent by nature, with no room for further questions, doubts or hesitation, and when you understand that all things are products, not only a lily flower but all things and phenomena, your naive impression of conditioned things being static or having room for a moment of stasis is defused and destroyed. Your awareness of something being impermanent automatically accompanies your awareness of that thing being a product.

Since everything, every object of the mind, whether material or immaterial, is a product, we need to keep in mind that everything is impermanent. We need to develop a deep understanding that absolutely everything is a product and therefore impermanent like lightning. We analyze the lily flower, and from that we make the leap from looking just at the lily flower to seeing everything, all other objects, as impermanent.

Meditation on Impermanence

Once you gain an understanding of impermanence by going through this analytical reasoning process, the only way to strengthen your awareness of impermanence is through meditation. In brief, meditation on impermanence is the process of mindfully and peacefully resting in the awareness of impermanence, without further analysis or conceptualization.

The awareness of impermanence is the awareness that all conditioned things can cease to exist at any moment due to the force of change within. Once we are able to gain and then to regain time and again that awareness through an analytical reasoning process, resting in that awareness without going through further analysis is called meditation on impermanence.

You might ask, "How do I know that I have arrived at the conclusion that all conditioned things can cease to exist at any given moment?" You can know whether you have arrived at this conclusion or not based on your ordinary impression of conditioned things as static or having room for stasis. If the ordinary impression that things are static or have room for stasis is intact, then the conclusion has not been reached. When that impression that things are static is gone or forced out, there occurs a new impression that conditioned things are not static.

When that new awareness occurs, then you have arrived at the conclusion that things are imminent to go out of existence in any given moment without need of any secondary causes or conditions. The object is imminent to go out of existence at any given moment without any secondary destructive force just because of its being a product. This is how you can know you have reached the correct conclusion and are properly meditating on impermanence.

Impermanence: Conclusion

In order to meditate on impermanence, first you must have a correct understanding of impermanence, gained through listening to the teaching, with dedicated discipline in studying and learning on your part. Second, you need to spend enough time contemplating and reflecting on the meaning of impermanence, as a means to solidify your understanding. Finally, you must meditate on impermanence by simply resting in the awareness of impermanence. Meditation on impermanence is the process of gaining personal familiarity with this newly gained awareness, until the awareness of impermanence becomes your second nature.

With this we have completed the teaching on impermanence and we will now turn to our other topic, the second subtle reality, emptiness.

Part Two: Emptiness

CHAPTER THIRTEEN

Introduction to the Teaching on Emptiness

ONCE YOU HAVE A good understanding and some experience meditating on impermanence, you are ready to begin studying emptiness. It is important to thoroughly understand the view of impermanence before attempting to understand emptiness, because the understanding of subtle impermanence helps you to see that all things and phenomena are very fragile in their nature. The quality of **fragility** helps prove or explain an object's emptiness because we can see that an object has no intrinsic stability at all. Moreover, as we have said, the mode of existence of all things can be understood at three levels of increasing subtlety: first, dependent arising, second, impermanence, and third, emptiness, the ultimate nature of all phenomena.

Attaining Happiness

Emptiness, or *shunyata* in Sanskrit, *tongpa-nyid* in Tibetan, is not just a dry esoteric Buddhist philosophical concept or teaching. The teachings on emptiness and the understanding or realization of emptiness strongly relate to our human quest for happiness. Since the realization of emptiness is very much relevant to our pursuit of happiness, we need to understand that teachings on emptiness are not just Buddhist philosophical concepts or teachings of interest only to egotistically elevated scholars. The realization of emptiness is one of the highest tools to attain true happiness, or what is called definite happiness.

In Buddhist teachings and scriptures, one frequently finds the term **two definite attainments** or **two definite goodnesses**. The first is the definite goodness of Nirvana, and the second is the definite goodness of Enlightenment. Nirvana and Enlightenment are considered to be definite attainments or definite goodnesses because once you attain those states, you cannot fall back. They are irreversible attainments and thus are called definite. To attain either Nirvana or Enlightenment, the realization of emptiness is indispensable.

Nirvana and Enlightenment are called the two levels of definite happiness or everlasting happiness. Nirvana is a personal liberation from *samsara*. Enlightenment is an omniscient mind characterized by universal compassion and wisdom, and so Enlightenment goes beyond Nirvana or personal liberation. The everlasting happiness of Nirvana and Enlightenment is ultimate, everlasting happiness that cannot be attained without removing or eliminating the seed of *samsara*. In his *400 Verses* **Aryadeva** says:

> *The seed of samsara ceases to exist in the moment when one sees the emptiness of all things and phenomena.*

Therefore, the realization of emptiness is the ultimate tool to achieve or to attain the everlasting happiness of Nirvana and the everlasting happiness of Enlightenment. As we have said, the teachings on emptiness or the realization of emptiness are very much related or relevant to our quest for real happiness.

Seed of Samsara

What does **Aryadeva** mean by "the seed of *samsara*"? The seed of *samsara* is the misconception or misperception of the ultimate nature of reality. This misperception gives rise to delusions. These delusions in turn give rise to emotional responses to the world around you, and negative actions follow. Delusions are the disturbing symptoms of the misperception of reality. This misperception of reality is deeply seated in our perceptual process. Misperception itself is not an obvious form of disturbance. However, the anger, jealousy, desire, lust, and so on that follow misperception of reality are very obvious to our mind as confusing and agitating. These inappropriate and disturbing emotional responses to the world around you instigate, motivate and manipulate your negative actions of body, speech and mind.

Through performing negative actions instigated by the negative emotions that arise when you are deluded or misperceiving the true nature of reality, you create karma. Unless you can eradicate the misperception of the ultimate nature of reality, you cannot get rid of these delusions. If you cannot get rid of delusions, you cannot stop creating karma. Between misperception, delusion and karma there is a sequential, causal relationship. When we fail to get rid of these three, then we automatically and involuntarily go through a vicious cycle of life, bound to pain and suffering. That vicious cycle of pain and suffering is called *samsara*.

Two Levels of Obstruction

In order to break the cycle of *samsara* and achieve both Liberation or Nirvana and Enlightenment, it is important to understand that there are two levels of obstructions. There are obstructions to Liberation and obstructions to Enlightenment. The obstructions to Liberation are karma and delusions. The obstruction to Enlightenment is our incorrect impression—due to the force of false appearance to our mind—that things and phenomena are intrinsically real. That misperception causes us to respond in a way that does not match with the true nature of things and phenomena. This means that our wrong impression acts as a hindrance to the omniscience of Enlightenment, which is knowing-without-thinking.

Impression and Belief

When a mirage appears to your mind as water, that very appearance of the mirage as water is wrong, false and deceptive. The wrong appearance of the mirage being water gives you an instantaneous impression that it is water. The false appearance of the mirage being water in your mind causes in you a belief that it really is water. Only the impression—that initial impression of the appearance of water—is the obstruction to omniscience or Enlightenment.

This is a little difficult. To our ordinary mind, first there is an impression, followed perhaps by a belief. One who has attained Nirvana naturally refrains from forming a belief based on a false impression. One who has attained Enlightenment spontaneously sees the truth of reality immediately without having any false impression.

These two, impression and belief, are different. If you have the impression of an appearance of water, an impression that water is there, it is not then necessary for you to form a conception of that water based upon your impression. You might realize that the appearance of water is due to a mirage, but in the case of belief, you have formed a conception of the water as really being there in relation to a mere image of water that, in fact, is wrong or mistaken with regard to the apprehended object.

If you do not carefully examine, impression and belief seem almost the same. If we do carefully examine, however, we understand that the very nature of what we call an impression and what we call a belief are two different things. An impression does not necessarily have the potential to lead to emotions. A belief has the potential to lead to actual emotions and negative actions.

There are three conditions needed for the formation of a mirage: light, heat and moisture. The image that arises from the meeting of these three conditions is called a mirage. The mirage gives an impression that water is there. Though that mirage appears to our mind as tangible or solid, there is nothing to be grasped or latched onto. It is just the appearance or image of water caused by the heat wave arising from the combination of the light, heat and moisture. That is all.

Under certain conditions, the image of water appears suddenly on the basis of a heat wave. When the image of the water pops up from that heat wave, it merely gives you an impression of its being water. That impression will not necessarily lead you to think or conceive of it as actual water. Simply due to the force of the arising image of water emerging from that heat wave, for a split second it prevents you from acting correctly. Your false impression prevents you from acting correctly in relation to the perceived object. This means, there is a momentary delay in your action due to a mismatch between your impression and the way the object really is. The type of impression that causes you to experience that delay through the force of deceptive appearance is called an obstruction to Enlightenment. When you train to eliminate the false impressions then you can reach Enlightenment.

Ordinarily, when you see a mirage, you have an impression of water and there is an immediate thought or conception or belief that the water actually exists, and this thought leads to emotional feelings like attraction, repulsion, etc. The actual emotions arising from the incorrect or wrong conception or belief will always manipulate, ignite or influence our actions of body, speech and mind to be unwholesome, destructive and negative.

If you find out that what you believed was real is actually not there, this brings you disappointment, frustration, anger, confusion or some kind of annoyance. All of these emotions are resulting from a belief, not just from a mere impression. Otherwise—if you could not avoid forming a belief based on your false impression—you could not eliminate the obstructions to Liberation before you eliminated the obstructions to Enlightenment. Remember, it is the conceptions and beliefs that are the obstructions to Liberation. The conceptions and beliefs are formed after the impression and you can attain Liberation by training in stopping the formation of beliefs—beliefs that are based on false appearances.

Next, it is important to understand the meaning of Enlightenment. As we have said, Enlightenment means omniscient mind or all-knowing mind. A state of mind that knows everything or anything spontaneously, without having the slightest hesitancy or hindrance to react in a match with the way things actually are, is an enlightened mind. There is no hindrance or hesitancy for that mind to know something without thinking—there is no false impression, so its knowledge is spontaneous and valid.

Therefore, the second type of obstruction, the obstruction to Enlightenment—the **incorrect impression** that causes a delay in perception and action—is definitely an obstruction to the attainment of an omniscient mind, because an omniscient mind knows everything or anything spontaneously without any hindrance or hesitancy to know, to respond and to act in a perfect match with the way things actually are.

Ordinarily your wrong impressions always cause your mind to delay in the process of correctly reacting or responding in a perfect match with the way things truly are. Something that causes you to delay acting appropriately is called a hindrance. That very subtle hindrance—false impression—is the obstruction to Enlightenment.

You cannot achieve or attain these two definite goodnesses, Nirvana and Enlightenment, without eradicating the two types of obstructions that we have just been describing. As part of the introduction to our full discussion on emptiness, there is some relevance to understanding the obstructions and in what order they must be eliminated.

Karma and *Klesha*

As we have said, there are two types of obstructions: obstruction to Liberation or Nirvana and obstruction to Enlightenment. Within the obstructions to Liberation there are two: karma, and delusions or *klesha*. Karmic obstruction, in brief, means the imprint of our own negative actions of body, speech and mind. Our negative actions are imprinted within our mind stream, or within the continuum of our mind. Each imprint of the negative actions of our body, speech and mind manifests or becomes active when it meets with the right conditions.

We say that the karmic imprint becomes active. Active means functionable or workable. In order for something to be activated, there must already exist something that has the potential to be activated. For example, when you apply for a credit card, have it approved and receive it in the mail, it must be activated before you can use it. You need to call the 800 number first, and they activate the card. Only then, when it is once activated, is it workable, usable or functionable to buy things at the grocery store. If you try to use a non-activated credit card, you will find it does not function; however, it does have the potential to function. That potential needs to be activated. Likewise, the imprints of our past negative actions of our body, speech and mind that are imprinted in our mind stream have potential and must be activated by meeting with the right causes and conditions. Once activated, they are fully capable of bearing their results.

Karmic Results

When your karmic seeds bring their results, you will experience those results in one of four ways, or in a combination of the four ways. You will experience them in your environment, in your actions and behaviors, in your actual experience or in your psycho-physical state.

When the results of negative karma manifest in your external environment, then the external world seems unpleasant and unattractive. Your environment feels like an inconducive place to live, very threatening to your well-being, protection, security and sustenance. This will occur no matter where you live. The location might change, but the problem will remain the same. No matter how you try to escape from one place to another, you will not find relief from this problem. There is almost no escape from this until that karma is exhausted.

When the results of negative karma manifest in your actions and behavior, then your actions are naturally negative, unwholesome, destructive, harmful and displeasing to others. You will have that natural tendency toward negative behavior, no matter how you try to avoid it. We are not saying it is impossible for you to get rid of that behavior. However, it is extremely difficult to reverse these tendencies. They can only be overcome through the long, gradual and painstaking process of training.

When the results of karma manifest in your actual life experience, then you will have a constant experience of conflict with your world. At the mental, emotional and psychological level, that experience of constant conflict between you and your world is always painful and unpleasant.

When the results of karma manifest in your psycho-physical state, then you will have either physical deformity or mental impairment from your birth.

The results of karma will manifest in one of those four forms, or in a combination of those four forms. Once you understand that, then you see that karma is definitely not destiny, not fate, not punishment imposed by a higher being or imposed by outside forces. Karma is the internal law of cause and effect, **internal** because the cause itself is created within your mental continuum, and the effect itself arises within your life experience, with no escape. That law of causality is called karma.

If you disregard karma then your future lives will be miserable. Right now, you are in the midst of a karmic life cycle, and by not understanding the law of karma you will continue to create millions of new karmic seeds, the causes for more unwanted results within what is already an undesired result created by a particular group of karmic seeds among the countless karmic seeds from your past lives. Within the cycle of the ripening of one karmic seed from the past, you are creating thousands of new karmic seeds.

Emptiness as Antidote

If you really think of the natural cycle of our life or consider it in that way, it can be very depressing. Falling into *samsara* is like falling into quicksand. The moment you fall into quicksand you can only sink. Because of one instant moment of movement, you sink faster. On the other hand, no matter how much negative karma or how many karmic seeds you have created, all of those karmic seeds can be wiped out within an instant moment of the realization of emptiness. So, there is hope. Not only hope; Enlightenment is actually achievable. The realization of emptiness is the most powerful antidote for the complete elimination of those two types of obstructions—the obstructions to Nirvana and the obstruction to Enlightenment.

Klesha

Remember we said that after karma, the second obstruction to Liberation or Nirvana is *klesha* or delusion. By definition, *klesha* means any type of thought or emotion that directly induces turmoil in your mental state. By their very nature, these *klesha* are incorrect reactions or responses to the outside, external or physical world. The physical world is the complex world of the five senses. You can or will have constant emotional reactions to whatever you see, hear, smell, taste or touch. The sense of sight, for instance, is the visual apprehension of anything that has characteristics of shape and color, and it is called form or *rūpa*.

Form and the other four—sounds, smells, tastes and touch—are the objects of the five senses. You can, or will, always have emotional responses to these objects, such as attraction, aversion, fear or confusion. All of these delusions or destructive negative emotions come from a misperception of reality and the unconscious habit of assenting in the false appearances. The underlying source, cause or seed of these emotions is the misperception of reality.

Misperception of Reality

For example, at night when you see a human image, you might mistakenly see that human image as a ghost. This perception is completely mistaken with regard to its apprehended object. This mistaken impression gives rise to fear, for example. The moment the fear arises or manifests in your mind, it creates or induces turmoil or agitation in your mental state. Likewise, whatever we see, hear, smell, taste or touch, always causes an inappropriate emotional response or reaction, such as attraction, repulsion, fear, confusion, anger, jealousy, and so forth, as long as we have this underlying misperception.

The moment these emotions arise in your mind, they create or induce turmoil in your mental state. The moment your mind is in that state of turmoil, your actions and behavior become unpleasant, negative and disharmonious. With your mind in turmoil you engage in inappropriate and harmful actions of body, speech and mind. Whenever you engage or indulge in any form of inappropriate harmful action of body, speech or mind, that action leaves a karmic imprint.

This is a very causal cycle—the misperception of reality leads to turmoil, namely negative emotions that are inappropriate emotional reactions towards the world. These inappropriate emotional reactions instigate, or motivate, your actions of body, speech and mind to be negative, unwholesome or disharmonious. Then, those unwholesome actions performed under the influence of delusion, which in turn has misperception as its underlying source, leave karmic imprints in your mind stream which will manifest sometime in the future. They will manifest when they meet with the right causes and conditions, and whenever those karmic seeds manifest upon meeting with the right conditions, they will bring their results in your environment, your actions and behaviors, your psycho-physical state or your very life experience.

Preciousness of the Human Form

As we said, that vicious cycle in which life somehow involuntarily rotates is called *samsara*. You are stuck in that regular recurring cycle of events, susceptible to pain and suffering in every moment. The only way to free yourself from this cycle is through realizing emptiness. **Aryadeva** said, in *400 Verses*:

> *There is no second door or gateway to ultimate liberation from samsara. The only door is through realizing emptiness.*

In general, all of the Buddha's teachings—whether *Sutrayana* or *Tantrayana* teachings, *Mahayana* or *Hinayana* teachings—directly or indirectly help you arrive at the full realization of emptiness. The ultimate goal of following the Buddha's teachings is to attain either of the two definite goodnesses, Liberation or Enlightenment. The happiness of Liberation and the happiness of Enlightenment are considered to be the highest, most reliable and irreversible forms of happiness that humans can achieve. **Shantideva**, in *A Guide to the Bodhisattva's Way of Life* explains:

> *Using this human form as a boat one can cross the ocean of samsara. Once we miss this boat, then it is very difficult for us to find another.*

This points to the preciousness or rarity of the human form. In all the *Lamrim* teachings, we find that the human form is rare, precious and meaningful. It is rare. This means it is difficult to obtain and it is attained very infrequently. It is precious and meaningful. Even though it is precious and meaningful, it is also easy to lose. It is fragile; its very nature is momentariness. Therefore, the realization of the preciousness and rarity of the human form gives us a sense of urgency to use it right away as a tool to achieve Liberation. **Shantideva** continues by saying:

> *Make sure not to fall into deep sleep in the darkness of ignorance.*

In other words, if you fail to make use of your human form, you will miss the boat. **Shantideva** encourages us not to waste this precious opportunity. The happiness of Liberation and Enlightenment are states of mind that only human beings can attain. One of our characteristics as human beings is that we have an intelligent mind, capable of exploring, ascertaining, experiencing or detecting the ultimate truth of reality, which lies beyond the deceptive appearance. The wisdom realizing emptiness is the only way in which we can eliminate our misperception of reality, the very source of our delusions or delusive emotions.

Chapter Fourteen

Prajnaparamita Sutra

As we said in the beginning, the realization of emptiness is very much related to our sincere quest for human happiness. Buddhist teachings on emptiness are not just philosophical exercises or teachings that are irrelevant to our human quest for happiness. They are completely necessary for the ultimate success of our quest for happiness. The Buddha taught directly in the *Prajnaparamita Sutra* about emptiness. *Prajnaparamita* means **perfection of wisdom**.

Great Tibetan Buddhist masters like **Lama Tsongkhapa** and his two heart disciples—**Gyalseb-jey** and **Khedrub-jey**—have written crystal clear commentaries on emptiness. Great Indian Buddhist masters like **Nagarjuna, Chandrakirti, Bhavaviveka, Aryadeva, Buddhapalita, Shantideva, Shantarakshita,** and **Kamalashila** have all written very extensive commentaries on emptiness based directly on the *Prajnaparamita Sutra*.

There are several different versions of the *prajnaparamita* or *Perfection of Wisdom Sutra*. For example, there is the *Sher-chin Bumpa*. *Bum* means 100,000; therefore, this is the *Prajnaparamita Sutra*, which has 100,000 stanzas. There is the *Nyer-tri*. This is the *Prajnaparamita Sutra* with 20,000 stanzas. Then there is the *Prajnaparamita Sutra* with 8,000 stanzas, the *Gye-tong-pa*. A fourth version, familiar to many, is the *Sher-chin Nyer-gnapa*. This is the *Heart Sutra*, the *Prajnaparamita Sutra* with 25 stanzas. A fifth is the *Sher-chin Yee-ghey Chic-ma*. This is the *Prajnaparamita Sutra* with simply one syllable, *Ah*. The *Ah* syllable conveys the full meaning of emptiness, just as effectively as the versions of the *Prajnaparamita Sutra* with one hundred thousand stanzas, twenty thousand stanzas, eight thousand stanzas, and twenty-five stanzas.

Often, fewer descriptive words will help to convey more, with less confusion. Too many words can cause the actual meaning to get lost or misinterpreted; at the end, all you may have is a headache, while the actual meaning has vaporized or become corrupted, contaminated. Therefore, giving a dense meaning, with fewer descriptive words, is one of the characteristics of a great author. A wise teacher has the ability to provide the greatest clarity with the least number of words.

All the direct teachings of the Buddha explain emptiness explicitly or implicitly. When the Buddha gave the *Heart Sutra* teaching, he remained in a deep meditative state. While in this state, he inspired Shariputra, one of his prime disciples, and Avalokiteshvara, the Buddha of compassion, to have a dialogue. Avalokiteshvara and Shariputra, engaged in effective dialogue deeply inspired by the Buddha. The way the discussion came out is like this—Shariputra asked how one should train in the perfection of wisdom, the *prajnaparamita*, the profound wisdom of emptiness. Avalokiteshvara answered:

> *View the five aggregates as empty of inherent existence. Form is empty, emptiness is form. Form is none other than emptiness, and emptiness, too, is none other than form. Similarly, feelings, perceptions, volition and consciousness are also empty of inherent existence."*

The five aggregates are form, feelings, perceptions, volition or compositional factors, and consciousness. Aggregate, or *skandha* in Sanskrit, means composite, pile or heap. Every knowable object, whether material or immaterial, substantial or non-substantial, falls in one of these five categories or aggregates. The *Heart Sutra* continues:

> *No eyes, no nose, no ears, no tongue, no body and no mental consciousness. Similarly, no form, no sound, no smell, no taste and no touch. In brief, all things and phenomena are empty of intrinsic existence and are empty of any substantial existence.*

"No eyes, no nose," and so forth refers to the lack of inherent existence of these phenomena. This means that in the ultimate sense, there is no inherent eye, no inherent ear, and so forth. None of the five aggregates exists inherently. They do not actually exist in the way they **appear** to our ordinary perception, as a reality. This is similar to our experience of "objects in the mirror are closer than they appear."

Those of you who drive a car are aware of this form of emptiness; there is a disparity between the way objects appear in your mirror and the way they actually are in terms of their reality. This is emptiness; it is that simple. For example, if you are driving a car with this awareness active in your mind, it prevents you from getting into an accident by thinking, "That car is very far away from me," and then changing lanes and immediately crashing into the other car. Rather, you are aware that the way the car appears in the mirror and the actual position of the car outside of the mirror are different; there is a disparity, or mismatch.

Similarly, "No eyes, no nose," etc. refers to the lack of inherent existence in all things and phenomena, not to any lack of conventional existence. Buddha was not saying that the eyes, nose, ears, tongue, body and mental consciousness do not exist. They all do exist, but on the conventional level, in an ordinary, actual, accepted manner. They do exist, on the conventional level, but they do not exist inherently; they have no intrinsic, independent existence. Things are **empty** of inherent existence; they are interdependent.

Commentaries on *Prajnaparamita*

Another way to help us understand the concept of emptiness is to learn from quotes from the treatises, which are reliable commentaries on the words of the Buddha. While these treatises are not made up of the actual words of the Buddha, they are written by highly realized teachers or masters. These most trustworthy commentaries are called *shastra* in Sanskrit, which means reliable treatises. Great Indian Buddhist masters like **Nagarjuna, Aryadeva, Chandrakirti, Shantideva**, and, in the Gelug tradition, Tibetan masters like **Lama Tsongkhapa** have commented on the Buddha's teachings on emptiness.

The greatest Indian Buddhist master, **Arya Nagarjuna**, was the primary founder of the *Prasangika-Madhyamika* philosophical school. He wrote an extensive and comprehensive commentary on the Buddha's teachings on emptiness. **Nagarjuna** explained logical methods for determining and understanding the meaning of emptiness. His *Six Famous Works* were profound commentaries on the Buddha's teachings on emptiness. One of these works is called *Mūlamadhyamākakārika, The Root Treatise on the Middle Way* or *The Root Treatise on Emptiness*. In this text, he expounds upon and attempts to reveal the true meaning of emptiness by stating:

> *Whatever is dependently arisen, that is explained to be emptiness. That being a dependent designation is itself the middle way.*

In another text, called *Ratnavalī*, or *Precious Garland*, **Nagarjuna** says:

There is no phenomenon that is not interdependently arisen.
Therefore, there is no phenomenon that is not empty.

Nagarjuna's closest inner disciple, **Aryadeva**, was like a son to him. **Aryadeva** also wrote a commentary on Buddha's teachings on emptiness; the text contains 400 stanzas and is therefore aptly titled *400 Verses*. In this text, he says:

Whatever is dependently arisen, must not have an independent status.
Since all things are dependently arisen, therefore, they must not have intrinsic existence.

400 Verses is the root text on which **Aryadeva** wrote a self-commentary, or *rang-drel* in Tibetan. In that text, he declares:

Things do not exist with substantial existence,
Like a coiled rope that exists as a snake
Only to the mind of the person who confusedly imputes
The name snake upon the coiled rope.

He explains how one might see a coiled rope and, out of confusion, believing he has seen a snake, assign the attributes of a snake to the innocent coiled rope. This person imputes a snake upon the coiled rope; however, the rope imputed as snake by the person who has the preconceived idea of snake is actually empty of any characteristics of a snake. It is only a rope.

Nothing exists with any substantial actuality or perceivable qualities within itself, just as there are no findable qualities of the snake within the coiled rope. The rope merely appears to be a snake because of our mistaken consciousness or perception. Similarly, all phenomena are devoid of any inherent characteristics that perfectly match the name, or designating term, given to them even if they are named in accord with conventional reality for conventional needs.

Chandrakirti wrote a text with ten chapters called *Madhyamakāvatāra*, or *The Entrance to the Middle Way*. In the sixth chapter, he says:

> *All things and phenomena are empty of inherent existence*
> *like a mirage and a magician's creation.*

Shantideva, in *Bodhicāryāvatara*, or *Guide to a Bodhisattva's Way of Life*, says:

> *Something that exists with inherent existence,*
> *What need is there for it to have a cause?*
> *Something that wholly exists,*
> *What need is there for it to have parts and fractions?*

Shantideva's statement points to these contradictions: If things come into existence due to causes and conditions, how could they have any inherent existence? If things come into existence with intrinsic existence, why do they need to depend on causes and conditions to come into being? This shows the obvious conflict in reasoning when it is asserted that although things are dependently arisen they have inherent existence.

The great Tibetan master **Lama Tsongkhapa** wrote a text called *Ten-drel Todpa, Praise to the Law of Interdependent Origination*, in which he says:

> *Dependent existence and independent existence are mutually exclusive.*
> *Since all things are dependently originated,*

Therefore, they are empty of independent existence.
No phenomenon is found to be intrinsically existent,
Since all things are dependent on something other than themselves.

These are all quotations that are to be found in the *shastra*, the most reliable commentaries on Buddha's words, written and compiled by highly realized masters or teachers. A *shastra* is a text that has been written by one who possesses the deepest knowledge and full realization of the topic under discussion. We will use quotations from the *shastra* as a reliable basis to discuss, study and expound emptiness in a more extensive way; from time to time, we will come back to these quotations.

We can find an abundant supply of books written by modern scholars, particularly western academic scholars. Most of these are written from a purely intellectual standpoint and lack the critical and vital component of realization on the part of the author. Therefore, regardless of how well written or inspiring we may find a particular book, it is better not to consider this type of work as *shastra*, since it lacks the critical component of realization on the part of the author. That does not mean we should consider them to be ordinary books, treating them without any sense of respect; rather, it is important to keep in mind the significant differences between *shastra* and books written merely at the academic level.

Interdependent Arising

At this point in the teaching on emptiness I would like to open a very brief discussion on interdependent arising. I will be presenting a fuller detailed discussion later on, under the five critical points for realizing emptiness.

The *Prajnaparamita Sutra*, Buddha's teachings on emptiness, deals implicitly with interdependent origination as the first and foremost evidence for emptiness. When the commentators on the

Prajnaparamita Sutra considered what the Buddha meant when he taught that form is void and so on, and they asked how it could be that all things are empty, they reached the understanding that things are empty because they are in fact interdependently arisen from impermanent ever changing causes and conditions and therefore have no intrinsic existence.

In the Buddha's own teachings, and in all the commentaries written by the great Indian and Tibetan masters, it is stated time and again that emptiness can only be understood within the context of interdependent arising or, in Sanskrit, *pratītyasamutpāda*. Without having a deep and complete understanding of interdependent arising, it would be extremely difficult if not impossible for us to understand the meaning of emptiness. All objects and phenomena are empty of inherent existence because they must rely upon something other than themselves in order to come into existence.

This is not saying that they are empty because they do not exist. They are empty just because of being interdependently arisen, just because they lack intrinsic existence. That all objects and phenomena come into being from and due to multiple impermanent causes and conditions (designation being one of these), indicates that they actually do exist. Therefore, in all the *sutra* and *shastra*, it is taught that emptiness must only be understood in the context of interdependent origination.

Without having a precise understanding of interdependent origination, it is impossible for us to comprehend the unmistaken, flawless meaning of emptiness in the way the Buddha intended. Sometimes in our own interactions with others, we may be misunderstood; our words can be misinterpreted, distorted, and lose their meaning. Our true intentions may not be realized. In the same way, when the Buddha was giving his teachings and said, "*shunyata*," without the hearers having a full understanding of *shunyata* or emptiness there was no way they could understand the true intention of his teaching. We must have a complete understanding of interdependent origination in order to understand the meaning of emptiness or *shunyata* according to the Buddha's intentions. If we do not have a clear view of interdependent arising, we are likely to form a wrong idea of the meaning of emptiness that would be damaging to our moral conduct.

As we just said, in order to understand emptiness we must first fully comprehend the meaning of interdependent origination, which is that nothing can arise without relying on some thing or things other than itself. Anything that comes into being is solely dependent on things or factors other than itself. Without relying or depending on something other than itself, there is no way for anything to come into being. It cannot come into being by its own nature, force, power, or by its own right. **Shantideva** said:

Something that exists with inherent existence, what need is there for it to have a cause?

He is asking: If something is able to come into being by its own nature, then why does it need to have a cause? This question directly negates the idea of intrinsic existence, thus proving the truth of interdependent origination. Objects and phenomena are entirely dependent on causes and conditions, parts and fractions, and designation; they actually do exist and function, yet only by being reliant upon other factors. They do not exist intrinsically but they do exist on the relative level, in dependence on other factors.

Interdependent origination means there is a dependent relationship between two things, or many things. Nothing can arise without relying on something other than itself. Therefore, the need of that thing is to rely on something other than itself, and therefore it cannot be independently arisen. For example, an old man cannot stand without relying on a walking cane. The only way he can stand is by relying, leaning, on that cane. Similarly, the only way something can arise is through relying on something else, on other factors, with no room for it to be independently arisen. This is the core meaning of interdependent origination.

It is vitally important to understand the meaning of interdependent origination deeply and fully, because interdependent origination serves as the powerful and indisputable evidence that all things are empty of inherent existence. Similarly, as we learned before in the lengthy teaching on impermanence, that any thing must be produced by impermanent causes and conditions serves as the powerful evidence that all conditioned things are impermanent and transient by nature. If you do not clearly understand this, your flawed idea of interdependent origination will not serve as evident proof that every phenomenon is both impermanent and empty, even while performing its conventional function. Now we can begin the detailed discussion of emptiness.

Chapter Fifteen

Critical Points to Understanding Emptiness

THE WAY WE ARE going to study emptiness in depth is through five critical points. In Tibetan, these are called *sa-ched*. *Sa-ched* are separate essential points which open further discussion aimed at understanding the main topic, in this case, emptiness. In the beginning it is good to state the five critical points briefly, and then we will treat each one separately at length.

The five critical points to understanding emptiness are:

- First, **interdependent origination**, which is the way all things exist interrelatedly or interdependently.
- The second critical point is the necessity to identify the **object of negation** and how to identify it. In Tibetan the object of

negation is *gagja*. *Gagja* means **that which is to be refuted, that which is to be negated,** or **that which is to be destroyed in order to cognize emptiness.** Without clearly identifying the object of negation, you cannot understand the real meaning of emptiness.

- The third of the five critical points is the statement that **the realization of emptiness arises as a mere detection of the absence of the object of negation** or *gagja*.
- The fourth critical point is how to posit the **conventional world** although all phenomena are empty. Conventional world means, for example, cups, pots, tables, and so forth, the things that we use in everyday life for our needs as well as all other objects of the mind. The conventional world is everything that exists conventionally as opposed to ultimately, or anything that exists for our needs and that we perceive by our ordinary mind. If we look for that object beyond our ordinary perception, we find that the object actually does not exist in the way we perceive. Having inherent existence is not its ultimate mode of being. However, an object that functions for our conventional needs exists conventionally, on the conventional level. In the wake of analysis the object does not exist in the way we see it; when we do not analyze we perceive objects as having intrinsic existence.
- The fifth and final critical point is how to **merge appearance and emptiness**. Appearance certifies conventional existence, and emptiness confirms its illusory nature. This is an extremely important statement. In our ordinary mind, these two views—appearance and emptiness—contradict. Appearance cancels something being empty, while emptiness cancels its appearance or functionality. It is extremely difficult for us to reconcile these two and bring them together by seeing that appearance and emptiness are two different aspects of the same thing. The full realization of emptiness is complete when we can merge the two

views and see that all things and phenomena are empty of inherent existence, yet fully capable to function. Then we are able to see appearance and emptiness as cohesive and complementary, with no room for conflict.

Chapter Sixteen

Critical Point One: Interdependent Origination

Now we will discuss the five critical points one by one and in more detail. As we said, the first critical point for understanding emptiness is interdependent origination. All the quotes from the *sutra* and *shastra* make it clear that emptiness and interdependent origination are two different aspects of the same phenomenon. An object's interdependent origination serves as the condition and basis for the inference of that object's emptiness of inherent existence. Therefore, all *sutra* and *shastra* agree unanimously through one voice that emptiness must be understood only in terms of the meaning of interdependent origination.

In Sanskrit, interdependent origination is called *pratītyasamutpāda*. In Tibetan, it is called *ten-drel*. The Tibetan word has two syllables: *ten* and *drel*. *Ten* means, **that upon which something depends.** *Drel* means, **interconnected, interrelated, interdependent.** So, the meaning of *ten-drel* is **that upon which something depends and that which it is dependent upon; between these two there is an interconnected relationship.** The interconnected relationship between them is the actual meaning of interdependent origination. *Ten-drel* describes or designates some object and that upon which it is dependent as having an interconnected relationship, as interrelated and interdependent for their mutual co-existence.

Buddha taught in the *Rice Seedling Sutra*:

Whoever sees interdependent origination,
Will also see emptiness.
Whoever does not see interdependent origination,
Will also not see emptiness.

And in the *Lam-tso Nam-sum* or *The Three Principal Aspects of the Path*, **Lama Tsongkhapa** said:

Though one has a full realization of Bodhicitta and renunciation, one cannot cut the root of samsara without having a realization of emptiness. Therefore, one should seek a correct understanding of interdependent origination through every means.

Like the lines from Buddha's teaching, this quote from **Lama Tsongkhapa** emphasizes the importance of gaining an understanding of interdependent origination as the key to understanding emptiness. The foremost interpreter of Buddha's teachings on emptiness, **Arya Nagarjuna**, said in *Prajnamūla* or *Root Wisdom, Fundamental Treatise on Emptiness*:

CRITICAL POINT ONE: INTERDEPENDENT ORIGINATION

Whatever is interdependently originated, that is to be explained as emptiness.

These quotations all emphasize and insist on the importance of interdependent origination as the key to realizing emptiness. Interdependent origination serves as the most powerful evidence and revelation that all things and phenomena are empty of intrinsic existence.

Three Levels of Subtlety

But, exactly what is the full meaning of interdependent origination? Going deeper, it is important to know that within interdependent origination, there are three levels of subtlety: first, interdependent origination in terms of cause and effect; second, interdependent origination in terms of parts and whole; and third, interdependent origination in terms of designation or imputation.

In Terms of Cause and Effect

Interdependent origination in terms of cause and effect refers to the unfailing interrelationship between one thing being a cause and the other being an effect. Such called **effect** cannot arise without depending upon a cause. The existence of the effect is heavily dependent upon its cause. Conversely, the existence of a cause is heavily dependent upon its effect. If something has no effect at all, by nature that thing cannot exist as a cause. Therefore, there is interdependence between these two.

For us, it is perfectly clear that an effect depends on a cause, but we might not think that a cause is also dependent upon its effect. We might think, "A cause must exist before its effect. If that is the case, how can the cause depend upon the effect, when the effect has not yet arisen?" For this reason, we might think a cause is not dependent upon its effect. But this is not the case.

The reason something is qualified as a cause is because it has a specific effect. Having an effect justifies the attribution of the term cause upon that phenomenon. Therefore, interdependence in terms of cause and effect does not simply mean **something produces something else**. That is not the full meaning of interdependence in terms of cause and effect. Similarly, having a cause qualifies something for the term effect to be imputed. These two phenomena—cause and effect—qualify each other. Whether the term is cause or effect, one serves as the qualifying factor for the proper designation of the other. That type of subtle interdependence to justify both terms—the term cause and the term effect — is interdependent origination in terms of cause and effect.

Our ordinary mind does not see that type of subtle interdependency between cause and effect. We only see that an effect is dependent on a cause. Without a cause, an effect cannot arise. Even if we see that the effect is dependent on the cause, we may not recognize the more subtle relationship of interdependency between cause and effect. Each justifies the other to be called cause or to be called effect.

In Terms of Parts and Whole

The second level of subtlety is interdependent origination in terms of parts and whole. In Tibetan, *cha* means parts, and *cha-chen* means **one that has parts**. So, *cha-chen* means **whole**. Parts are the necessary basis which justifies the designation whole upon that set of parts. Similarly, the existence of the whole is what justifies the designation part of the whole. For example, there cannot be a table leg if there is no table for the leg to be a part of. There is an unfailing interdependency between parts and the whole.

We are not only saying that when parts are hooked together there is a whole. This is simply a collection of parts. Parts are a necessary factor for the formation of the whole, but this is only one side of the interdependency. Parts are the essential basis to justify the term whole to be designated upon that set of parts, and similarly, the whole is the essential basis to justify the term parts which is designated upon its fractions.

That type of interconnection or interdependency, in which parts are the essential need for the formation of the whole and the whole is the essential need for the formation of the parts, is more subtle than the ordinary perception of dependency between parts and whole. It is easy to understand that parts make the whole. The whole is more than just a collection of parts. Whole means that which serves as the indispensable basis for the designation of the term parts. Similarly, parts means those which serve as an indispensable basis for the designation of the term whole. This is the only mode through which such things called parts and such a thing called whole come into being. There is absolutely no way for parts or whole to come into being without having a mutual dependence.

We should not take this to mean, **parts are the cause for the whole**. Even though the existence of the whole depends on parts, the parts are not the cause of the whole. First, if the parts would be the cause of the whole, as soon as the whole comes into being the parts would cease, as when a seed transmutes into a plant and is no longer there as a seed; secondly, the parts form the whole but do not produce the whole. In general the whole is a collection of its parts. The parts can be disassembled and there is no whole. Between parts and whole there is an interdependent relationship, but this type of interdependent relationship is not a causal dependent relationship. Therefore, parts are not the cause of the whole, and the whole is not the effect of the parts. However, these two do have an interdependent relationship. Without existence of parts there cannot be existence of whole, and vice versa. The existence of the whole is only in reference to the parts and vice versa; without reference to each other, there is no existence, as there is no existence of short without reference to long.

That all things are interdependent for their existence indicates that they do not have intrinsic or substantial existence. Nothing is self-characterized to be a cup, to be a table, to be a cause, to be an effect, etc. Nothing is self-characterized to be parts or to be whole. In fact a whole can be identified only by depending upon its parts. In order to be seen as a whole, that phenomenon must be dependent upon something such as its parts or fractions. This means there is no way to see something as a whole without its being composed by fractions; to see something as a whole, you must identify a set of parts.

For instance, when we see a table, can we see that table without relying on seeing any of its parts? No; we cannot identify a whole without having implicitly identified at least some of its parts. Identifying a whole depends on identifying its parts. If we cannot distinguish its parts, there is no way to establish it as a whole. There is no way to establish the whole without implicitly distinguishing its parts. This indicates that anything called a whole does not have a self-generated identity of wholeness; congruently, any things called parts do not have self-generated identities of partness. If parts did have a self-generated quality of partness which has nothing to do with the existence of the whole, then these parts could be identified without relying on the identification of the whole. Similarly, the whole could be recognized without relying on identifying the parts.

We tend to see things such as a table leg as standing on their own, as somehow having an independent, self-generated existence or integrity even if we see them as part of a whole. Here is the table leg; it seems to be inherently existent as a thing, a piece of wood. If we reflect on our experience, however, we find that this assumption about self-generated qualities is invalid. It cannot be the case; it is impossible. The table leg itself is in a sense a whole which has its own parts and so on. This leads us to conclude that there is a coherence, an interdependence, between these two phenomena, parts and whole. Without one the other cannot arise or have any identifiable characteristics. They are both self-essenceless. They have no self-generated or self-produced identity, and therefore, they are empty in nature.

CRITICAL POINT ONE: INTERDEPENDENT ORIGINATION

In Terms of Imputation or Designation

This leads us to the third level of subtlety, which is interdependent origination in terms of imputation or designation. This is the most subtle level. In addition to being interdependently arisen in terms of cause and effect and in terms of parts and whole, anything that exists as an object of the mind is dependent on a name, or term, given to it by a designating conceptual mind. Nothing can exist independently from an imputing mind or consciousness. Nothing has a substantial force or essence which qualifies it to exist on its own; it must rely on the process of us giving it a name.

This is not the same as the mind-only, or *Chittamatra* school of Buddhism where everything exists as a mere reflection of the mind. Here we are saying that there is an interdependent relationship between the term imputed by our mind and that upon which the term is imputed. The relationship should one of cohesive and concordant interdependency.

When the mind or consciousness assigns a name to something, that name is called a designation. The technical term for the object upon which the term is applied is the **basis of imputation**. The mind imputes a term upon an object. It is very important to realize and to remember that that object—the object upon which the term is imputed—is not the term. This is so important I will say it again right here—The basis of imputation or designation is not the term.

An object to which the mind gives a name does not suddenly become, or change into, that term which the mind has applied or assigned. Nor has it existed before as what it is now named. Instead, any object is caused to exist—for example as a cup—through designation, in order to fulfill our conventional needs. There is nothing to be found as cup at its substantial level.

The classic example of this point is from **Aryadeva**, and so I will repeat the quote from his *rang-drel* or self-commentary on the root text *400 Verses*:

Things do not exist with substantial existence,
Like a coiled rope that exists as a snake
Only to the mind of the person who confusedly imputes
The name snake upon the coiled rope.

The process of imputing snake on a coiled rope and the process of imputing snake on a real snake are exactly the same. At first, this assertion may be extremely difficult for us to understand. At first, we may not see that in both cases, the term snake is imputed upon something which is non-snake in the sense that neither object exists inherently. Snake and rope as objects of the mind are empty of inherent existence.

We realize that when we perceive the coiled rope to be a snake, we may feel strong emotions and even have the physical signs of fear, nervousness or repulsion that arise when we see a "real" snake. From this we understand that in one case the term and the basis of the imputation are cohesive and concordant while in the other case, they are incohesive and inconcordant.

No matter how much you impute snake onto a coiled rope, it will never function as a snake in the conventional world. This means that even though the rope temporarily takes on the appearance of a snake due to your mistaken perception, that snake will never be able to perform the function of a snake in the conventional world. However much its appearance may prompt emotions to arise as though it were an actual snake, it can never slither over and bite you. This is due to the inconcordant relationship between the term you gave it and the actual basis of designation. You called it a snake but it was only a coiled rope. When we apply the term snake to a coiled rope, the mind that applies that term is mistaken and confused, and the term is "incorrect," that is, not concordant on the conventional level. It is important to understand that a term or name applied to an object might not be coherent or concordant—the relationship between name and object in the case of calling a rope a snake is incoherent and inconcordant.

When there is a mismatch, then the misapplied term can cause us agitation, as when we feel fear when we see a rope as a snake.

As we have said, the term is not the same as the basis of designation. This is shown clearly by the example of mistakenly designating a rope as a snake. If the basis of the designation would actually exist as the term—would be identical to the term—then there would be natural logical consequences. For example, if a certain object would be a clock, there would have to be a defining set of physical characteristics that would qualify the object as a clock and that would demand that the object be identical with the term clock. But if we consider, we all know the difference between an object and a term; we usually just do not think about it. If the set of physical characteristics upon which we are going to impute the term clock already exists as a clock, then you would have to assert that there is clock-ness in that object. If that which we are going to call clock is already a clock, then we do not need to give it that name because it already exists as a clock by its own force. When we **identify** an object as a clock, we make the mistake of thinking it already exists as a clock, and we are only giving it the right name.

Our ordinary mind mistakenly views the term and the basis of imputation as the same thing or identical. Therefore, we always have the comfortable reliable impression of clock-ness in the clock. But the basis of imputation cannot and must not be identical with the term. If the basis is the term, then a clock already exists within its substantial components before we can apply the term clock. In actuality, this is not the case.

Neither clock nor clock-ness exists anywhere within the object's characteristics before we provide that name. From the very moment we name those components clock, that set of elements exists as a clock only because of our designation. It still lacks clock-ness. When there is concordance between the term and the object upon which the term is imputed, the way we name something will never fail to fulfill our purpose in giving it that name. On the other hand, between the term snake and the coiled rope, there is no concordance or harmony. When a coiled rope is called a snake, it of course cannot function as a snake. The purpose of applying snake to rope is defeated.

It is extremely important to understand this third and most subtle level of interdependent origination—imputation or designation—in order to be able to proceed to the second critical point, which is how to identify the object of negation or *gagja* in Tibetan. If we still think that the basis of designation is the same as the term, we will never be able to identify the *gagja*. If we do mistakenly think of the object as the same as the name we give it, our idea can be proven false or erroneous as we have been showing.

Ordinarily things appear to our mind as being the same as their name, which convinces us of the existence of clock-ness in the clock. We think that having clock-ness, is the only way something is able to exist as a clock, and this notion serves as the basis for all types of disturbing emotions and psychological distress.

As we have described, interdependent origination in terms of imputation or designation involves the process of naming something, for example a snake, rope, cup, chair, table, carpet, door, window, kitchen, etc. The name, correctly or not, is imputed upon a basis of imputation. Anything we can see, hear, smell, taste or touch, as well as anything that can be ascertained by our mind, is dependent upon conceptual imputation for its existence.

It is now time to review and restate the first critical point for understanding emptiness, namely interdependent origination and its three levels of subtlety, especially the third and most subtle level, which is imputation.

Whether it is physical reality, mental reality or abstract phenomena, all things are dependent upon conceptual imputation for their existence. Without relying on the process of imputation, nothing can exist as a cup, table, chair, and so forth. Things and phenomena do not have their own self-characterized nature that validates their existence as a cup, as a table, and so forth. Therefore, all things and phenomena must depend upon conceptual imputation for their existence.

A clock does not exist as a clock to us until we designate some object as a clock. Unless you impute the term clock onto some basis, it cannot exist for you as a clock. This object, with its distinguishing set of physical characteristics such as color, shape, size, location, minute and hour hands and so forth, cannot exist as a clock unless you name it as a clock. This is because the object that you name clock does not have any self-characterized essence, or being, that proves its own existence as a clock. Thus, this object has a completely dependent nature. We must assign the name clock for it to exist as a clock. As we have said, this is the most subtle meaning of interdependent origination.

Rope and Snake

Now we will return to the example of the rope and the snake. As we said, this is the classic illustration of interdependent origination in terms of imputation or conceptual designation. The great scholars **Nagarjuna, Chandrakirti** and **Lama Tsongkhapa** all agree that the mode of imputation of snake to a real snake and the mode of imputation of snake to a coiled rope are exactly the same in that there is no inherent snake-ness in either rope or snake to demand that you give it the name snake beyond your choice. Please notice the key word here, **inherent**. Both the coiled rope and the live snake lack inherently existing elements to signify that the object must exist only as a snake. In fact no object has intrinsic qualities. Any object, whether snake or rope, necessarily arises or forms from a wide variety of factors, from multitudinous factors. In the case of the rope, there are most obviously the farmer who grows the hemp plant, the harvested hemp itself, the one who turns the plant into fibers, the weavers of the rope, and so forth. In the case of the snake, it does not spring up whole but results, like every other object, from ever changing impermanent factors, so many that the process defies enumeration. If we think about this we will see that everything is part of an infinite process. Our mind projects on to the universe, picking out what to objectify and name.

So, both the coiled rope and the live snake lack intrinsic elements to signify or demand that the object must exist only as a snake. Therefore, in terms of the mode of imputation, these two objects are identical with regard to how they were assigned the name snake. These two objects are both sets of parts that can accept a name although no part has inherent existence. No part demands or requires the name snake. This is a deep point.

To repeat, when you impute snake to the coiled rope, the rope does not have any inherent quality which receives or requires the name snake. In the same sense, when you impute snake to a real snake, the snake does not have any inherent receiving quality that requires that name snake. Neither the real snake nor the coiled rope has any receiving quality requiring the imputation. At the very objective level, they are both absent of any inherent quality that requires them to receive the name snake. Each is the product of innumerable impermanent ever changing factors. Each is empty of inherent existence.

Concordance

If only the naming of a snake validated the existence of the object as a snake, then both term and named object would function as a real snake. Since neither the rope nor the snake has an objective quality that requires that it receive the name snake, there must be something more that is required than just the name, since only one of the two objects can, on the conventional level, perform the functions of a snake. Therefore, whatever name or term we impute on something, that something, the basis of designation, must be concordant with the term we give it in order to function in the conventional world as we intended. There must be a **valid** basis of imputation that is concordant with the imputed name or term.

The term valid basis itself is somewhat problematic because it only appears in Tibetan commentaries and not in any of the reliable Indian texts. In **Lama Tsongkhapa's** texts, the term appears very rarely. So, there is some controversy about valid basis. Here we will prefer to use the term **concordance**. For the object we name to function on the conventional level in the way we intend, there must be natural concordance between the term and the basis upon which that term is designated.

Since the name is not the same as the object, whatever term we designate upon something is not the way for that object to exist. The term we apply to an object may not be concordant, as in the snake/rope example. The term does not demand that the object exist in the way we name or the way we intended. In other words, the object itself does not demand that we give it that term and that term does not demand that we apply that term to that object. So, in **Lama Tsongkhapa** and some other Tibetan texts it says there needs to be a valid basis of imputation; but as we just said, that term valid cannot be found in any reliable Indian literature. This is why many great Tibetan masters are reluctant to use that term valid. However, whether we use the term valid or not, we all feel that there needs to be natural concordance between the term and the object upon which it is imputed for the object to function as intended by the designator.

Regarding the technical terms **imputation** and **basis of imputation**, there must be a natural concordance between the term and the object upon which the term is imputed in order for the object to function as intended by the designator. If this would not be the case, if there would be no need for a natural concordance between the term and what the term is imputed upon, then there would be no reason at all why a coiled rope cannot exist or function as a snake after being named as a snake. We all know that a coiled rope cannot function as a real snake. So, this shows that there must be a natural concordance between the term and what the term is imputed upon for the object to function as understood and intended by the designator.

Because we see that natural concordance is necessary for an object to function in accordance with the name we give it, we understand that it is not the process of designation that creates the functionality of a clock or a snake, so and so forth. We understand that the process of naming alone is not what brings that object into existence with a particular function. Whoever the designator, whatever the process of designation, whatever the term might be and whatever it is imputed upon, between the term and whatever it is imputed upon there must be concordance. The object should exist and function in accordance with the term and the designator's intention.

However, to repeat, whatever concordant term that we impute upon something is not the means for the object to exist with its functionality in a match with the term and the intention of the designator.

As we have said, the process of imputation is the process of giving a name to something. Moreover, the object upon which the term is imputed is not the same as the imputed name. The basis of imputation and the imputed name are not one. They are not identical. The imputed name is not the same as the basis of imputation, and the basis of imputation is not the same as the imputed name. These two are separate. Therefore, the process of imputation is not a means for making something become one with the term. Indeed, there is no way to make something become one with the term!

There are three ways to state this. You might say, the process of naming does not mean making that phenomenon to be the same as the term. You could say, the process of imputing a term upon something is not the process of making that phenomenon in the same nature of the term. Or you could say, the process of imputation is not the process of making something one with the term.

Most people confuse the name with its object. All of their three common assumptions—that naming makes an object the same as the name, in the same nature as the name, or one with the name—are incorrect understandings of the process of imputation. Unless we clearly understand designation—the third and most subtle level of interdependent origination—then there is no way for us to go on to the second critical point, which is to identify the object of negation, the *gagja*. Therefore we will now review once more.

Review of the Process of Imputation

It is vital to understand interdependent origination, the way all things exist interrelatedly or interdependently, as the first of the five critical points for understanding emptiness. The necessity to identify the object of negation or *gagja*, in Tibetan, is the second critical point. If we understand the role that interdependent origination—specifically imputation—plays in the existence of an object as a cup, as a table, and so forth, we can proceed to the second critical point. Unless we have a precise and deep understanding of the process of interdependent origination and imputation, it is unlikely that we will be able to identify what needs to be negated in order to confirm an object being empty.

This subject is very difficult. In the monastery, we study interdependent origination for four years as full-time students, memorizing the root text, memorizing the commentaries on the root text, receiving oral teachings from a teacher, and then engaging in rigorous debate for hours and hours to analyze the day's teaching and concretize the understanding of the process of imputation. As a result of debate, one's understanding of the process of imputation becomes clearer and clearer, deeper and deeper, and more and more solid with less room for confusion.

Finally, you will have real conviction. You will have a doubtless understanding which functions in your meditative practice, and you really start seeing the process of imputation without having to re-analyze the whole process. And, that understanding will open a new door to see a new and fresh reality.

You realize that the process of imputation is not the process of re-naming. For instance, in the beginning you might think that a clock already exists within its material components, and you are just re-naming it as a clock. The naive feeling that hangs out in your mind is that there is something within the object that already exists as a clock that is only made apparent due to naming.

Gradually you realize that first, the process of imputation is not the same as the process of making that phenomenon one with the name. Second, the process of imputation is not the same as simply re-naming something that is already there. Third, the process of imputation is not the process of making the phenomenon in the same nature as the term. Keep these three in mind. These three tell what the process of imputation is not. Understanding what the process of imputation is not will help you to understand what the process of imputation actually is.

Regarding the process of imputation or designation, in order to designate a concordant term upon something, there are several requirements. First, there must be a conventionally healthy and rational designator, one who is absent sickness which damages either the sense organs or the mind, absent insanity, absent damage to the sense organs, and absent external obstruction. One who is hallucinating might want something that he does not need. He starts seeing something when there is nothing to be seen, and then he names that: "Oh, there is something there. I'll call it water. I'll call it cup. This is cup." This disqualifies him as a rational designator. Second, there must be a designating term. Third, there must be a concordant basis of designation. And fourth, there must be an intention to designate based on conventional needs.

These four must be present in order to qualify the process of imputation as valid. However, the mode of imputation is the same in all cases.

The reason why a coiled rope cannot function as a snake even after being named snake is because of the interference of illusion. You named a coiled rope as a snake due to the interference of confusion. A coiled rope appears to your mind as a snake because of several of its characteristics: The rope is coiled the way a snake is coiled; there are

Critical Point One: Interdependent Origination

some resembling shape, color and texture. Also, your mind has the generic image of snake. Because these characteristics of the rope match your generic image of a snake, you name the rope, "A snake!" As we have seen, the process of naming a real snake is exactly the same, but the reason why the coiled rope does not exist as a snake and function as a snake—even though you named it as a snake—is because of the interference of illusion. You have seen a snake where there is only a rope. This proves that your designation is not in any way the same as the basis of designation.

Rope does not have anything in it which qualifies it to be snake. Similarly, a live snake does not have anything in it—any inherent quality—which qualifies it to be a snake or demands that it be a snake either before or after naming. Both rope and snake are absent any inherent characteristics.

Rope does not have any physical characteristics of snake. A coiled rope resembles a snake under certain circumstances, but it does not have characteristics of a snake at the conventional level. A "real" snake, while it has the features of a snake at the conventional level, also does not have any substantial or inherent characteristics of snake or anything else, in exactly the same way that rope does not have any material or substantial characteristics either of snake or of rope within itself which simply need to be named.

As we have also seen, in both cases, there is nothing out there on its own which needs to be simply re-named as a snake. Then the question comes, "Why? If that is the case, then real snake should not exist as a snake, and if that is the case then why shouldn't a rope exist as a snake? If neither rope nor snake has any material, substantial or inherent qualities of snake which simply need to be re-named, then how can we understand or name anything?" This leads us to the second critical point—but first we need to summarize the first critical point, interdependent origination, yet again, to strengthen our understanding.

Summary of Interdependent Origination

We have finished a lengthy presentation of interdependent origination, the first critical point for understanding emptiness. The most subtle meaning of interdependent origination is that for anything and everything to exist, for example as a snake, rope, cup, table, chair, pen, living room, bedroom, kitchen and so forth, it is solely dependent on a conceptual designating term. The objects themselves do not have any inherently substantial, material or physical characteristics of snake-ness, cup-ness, table-ness, chair-ness, etc. There is no cup-ness that is already there within an object's components which simply needs to be re-named through designation. Therefore, everything that exists as a cup, as a table and so forth is solely dependent on conceptual designation. Therefore, nothing exists to you as a cup or as a table unless you label it as a cup or as a table.

This is the way all things and phenomena come into being. They do not come into being because of a force that exists on their own side, through their own power, or under their own right. Once we have a correct understanding of interdependent origination—in terms of cause and effect, parts and whole, and designation—then, whenever we perceive the object cup, the awareness of the object cup itself triggers the instantaneous understanding that the cup is dependently existent and not independently existent.

Ideally, that awareness would in turn trigger the understanding that the object is dependent solely on the ascription of a term to a basis of imputation, and that the object is not a base projecting a characteristic that includes its name or identity. There is a term employed to designate a base, and that base itself has no inherent characteristics which make it what it is. The base itself does not have its own self-characerized identity. The base may be **valid** because it is **concordant** with the designation—but the base has no inherent quality. All its apparent characteristics are illusory; they seem to exist independently, but in fact they are interdependently arisen.

Critical Point One: Interdependent Origination

This is the very essence of the teaching on the three levels of interdependent origination. The first level is interdependent origination in terms of cause and effect. The second is interdependent origination in terms of parts and whole. The last one is interdependent origination in terms of designation. To repeat—Unless we have a correct and deep understanding of interdependent origination, there is no way to proceed to the second critical point, the object of negation, the *gagja*.

Once we have the thorough correct understanding of interdependent origination, whenever we see an object—for instance, a cup—seeing that object cup triggers the awareness that the designating term and the basis of imputation are fundamentally not the same. The valid basis itself does not have the slightest bit of self-characterized identity. The validity of the base is not dependent upon it having some inherent characteristic which makes it what it is. Through this understanding, we can see the disparity between the way things appear to be and the actual mode of their existence.

Chapter Seventeen

Critical Point Two: The Object of Negation

ONCE WE HAVE THAT thorough understanding of the first critical point, interdependent origination, and especially of the mode of imputation, the most subtle level of interdependent origination, we can proceed to the next step, identifying the object of negation, called *gagja* in Tibetan. The object of negation is the second critical point.

You will find a lot of repetition in this teaching on the second critical point, the *gagja*, because this is a difficult subject, and to consolidate understanding it is necessary to go over the explanation again and again.

To start, you might ask, "Just what is the object of negation?" The answer is that it is the false appearance of any object you name that directly contradicts the actual mode of existence of the object. That false appearance of a thing that directly contradicts its true mode of existence is the object of negation, and it needs to be identified and then negated, refuted, disqualified and stopped from appearing so that we can detect the actual reality which is always obscured by that false appearance. In order to help us get an idea of the *gagja* we use the analogy of a mirage.

Mirage: An Analogy to the *Gagja*

When a mirage appears to your mind as water, the mirage appearing to your mind as water is a false appearance. This is the same as the false appearance of any object that appears to your mind as inherently real. The mirage appears to your mind as water, and that very appearance of the mirage being water contradicts the actual mode of existence of the mirage and contradicts the very fact of what exists out there in reality. What exists out there is a mirage, which we know is a deceptive appearance. Neither the mirage nor any of its elements is inherently existent. All these are interdependently arisen. The mirage is a mere appearance.

A mirage can appear as a mirage even to an enlightened mind. An enlightened mind sees a mirage and knows it is a mirage because for the enlightened mind there is no disparity between the appearance and one that appears. For some reason, however, when we see a mirage, what appears to our naive mind is water. So, the appearance of the water contradicts what is really out there in conventional reality. Similarly, like a mirage, the object of negation or *gagja* is the false appearance as inherently existent of anything and everything. This false appearance directly contradicts the actual mode of existence of objects. Their actual mode of existence is that they arise, abide and cease interdependently, in interaction with other ever changing factors and not through independent force.

Unless we are able to identify the false appearance of the object that directly contradicts its actual mode of the existence then there is no way for us to identify the object of negation, for the object of negation IS this false appearance, this appearance of things as solid or existing by their own power. When we cannot clearly identify the object of negation, then there is no way to negate that false appearance through a counteracting analysis. We want to negate the false appearance and so we must clearly identify the *gagja* or object of negation.

The easiest way to explain the object of negation is that it is the inherent existence of all things and phenomena. However, between the two ways of explaining the object of negation given here, the first one gives more information. This first one is a little complicated: The object of negation is the false appearance of anything and everything, that directly contradicts the actual mode of existence of that object. The second one—inherent existence—is easy to express, easy to remember and easy to explain, but, at the same time, it gives you very little information on what the object of negation really is. The first definition may seem a little confusing in the beginning, but it is more detailed and gives you more information. It explicitly conveys the full meaning of the object of negation by showing that there are two parts to the definition: one, the false appearance of the object; and second, that which contradicts the actual mode of existence of the object.

Five Questions to Understand How We Normally Perceive

We need to understand how we habitually perceive things as if all things and phenomena exist by their own power or by their own nature or in and of themselves without being interdependently arisen, without relying on designation. We see them as somehow existing independent of their designated name. To help understand how we ordinarily perceive, there are five questions we should ask ourselves about the false appearance of the object clock:

1. Does the object clock appear to my mind as being inherently existent as a clock?
2. Does the object clock appear to my mind as existing in and of itself as a clock?
3. Does the object clock appear to my mind as complete in and of itself, as having clock-ness?
4. Does the object clock appear to my mind as being something more than a basis of designation, something more than an object that I have named clock?
5. Does the object clock appear to my mind as existing as a clock at its very substantial level, giving the impression that it is locatable within its parts or whole?

We should carefully consider these five questions in order to see the mismatch between the way things appear and the way things actually are. Things normally appear to our mind in one or more of these five ways, and then we assent to that false appearance as the fact of reality, just as when a mirage appears to our mind as water, we assent to that false appearance of water as the fact of reality, believing that water is actually there.

Whenever you assent to the reality of false appearance, it will always serve as a cause for mental, emotional and psychological pain. For example, if you have a need for water to relieve your thirst and you assent to the false appearance of a mirage being water—believing that it is real water and then approaching the location of that appearance confident that you will find water—you will not find any water where you believed it to be. Instead of making you calm, peaceful and happy, the experience of not finding water where you believed it to be agitates, frustrates, disappoints and angers you. When that happens, will you blame the mirage or will you blame your delusions? You will blame the mirage; we always blame the innocent, rather than the guilty.

Before learning about the object of negation in great detail, we must pay mindful attention to how we normally perceive things and how things normally appear to our mind. We must try to gain some sense that there is a mismatch between how things appear to our mind and how things really are.

Right now, we do not see that there is a disparity between those two. We have a strong feeling that things really exist in the way they appear, and that things exist in the way we perceive. We assume, "Things should exist in the way they appear, and things should exist in the way I perceive them!" First, we have to identify this kind of habit and make ourselves more inclined to see things as they really are, rather than simply believing in the way things ordinarily appear to us.

How do things appear to our mind that contradicts their actual mode of existence? Things appear to our mind as existing, for example, as a clock, without depending on the process of conceptual designation for their existence. Which means, when you are in a non-analyzing or naive state, an object appears to your mind as existing as a clock in and of itself without depending upon your conceptual designation for it to exist as clock. The object that we call a clock appears to our mind as substantially, materially or objectively existing without the need of a consciousness to perceive and designate it.

So, you see an object as existing in itself without any need for you designating it subjectively. When you are not judging or analyzing at all—when you are not thinking, "Is this, is it not? Should this, should this not?"—the object appears to your mind as existing as a clock without depending upon the need of conceptual designation for its existence. We see it as objectively existing as a clock without the need of subjective interference for it to exist as a clock, and we do not recognize the object that we call clock as interdependently arisen, as a product of countless impermanent ever changing causes and conditions, including our designation of it as clock.

We use the clock as an example, but we view everything this way. We are very much convinced that this is how all things and phenomena actually exist. However, as we learned before in the discussion of interdependent arising in terms of imputation or designation, without subjective interference nothing can exist as a clock, as a table, as a chair, so and so forth. Nothing exists under its own power, by its own force or under its own right. Being inherently, objectively existent as a clock would mean that the clock would exist without the need of a designating consciousness and designating term and, we know from studying interdependent arising that this is impossible.

The deeper we go into this subject, the more intricate the subject of the *gagja* or object of negation becomes and the more perplexed the students become. There are no clues like sounds and smells which help you identify the meaning of the subject. So, now you become a stranger in an old place. It is okay to be a stranger in a new place, but now you have become a stranger in an old place—a place that you thought was familiar. That is dangerous.

First, it is very important to see how things normally appear to our mind. Secondly, it is important to see if the way things normally appear to our mind contradicts the actual mode of existence of things and objects. Thirdly, it is important to become familiar with this new view of reality and become distant from our old habitual way of seeing things and objects. It is very difficult to do these three things.

Once we recognize how things appear to our mind now, we will be ready to consider new answers to the five questions. Right now we would have to answer "Yes" to all five questions. If we recognize how things appear to our mind, we would have to answer yes, because now things do appear to our mind in all five ways. When we understand how things appear, we can then consider that a "No" answer should be correct. When we fully recognize that now we would answer yes to all the five questions, then deeper teachings on the object of negation will make things clearer for us rather than more perplexing. Which means, instead of making your mind numb, deeper teachings should crystallize your understanding.

Teachings on the object of negation should not be like a drug where the more you take, the more you become numb and then you identify that numbness as blissfulness. You do not want to become totally numb and then see that numbness as a peaceful state. The teachings on the object of negation should not numb you at all. What really keeps you from becoming numb during teachings on the object of negation is recognizing that you would now answer yes to those five questions about how things appear to you, and at the same time realizing that this appearance of things is deceptive.

How to Identify the Object of Negation

To review briefly—The way to begin to identify the object of negation is first to carefully examine how things and phenomena appear to your naive, un-analyzing mind, to examine how you would answer those five questions we asked before. For instance, now a clock appears to your naive mind as existing at its very substantial level, or it appears to be locatable within its substantial constituents. It appears to your mind as possessing a clock-ness within it that demands the name clock beyond your needs and choice. We think that this object exists as a clock, because, regardless of what we call it, it already exists as a clock at its substantial level and simply needs to be re-named through applying a label.

First, we need to realize "Yes, this is how objects ordinarily appear to my mind. This is how I respond, how I relate, and this is what I believe to be the clock's mode of existence." We always assume that there is something within the object which makes it a clock, and that this is the only manner in which it comes into being.

Unless we really recognize how things appear to our naive and un-analyzing mind, then it is not possible for us to be able to identify the object of negation. Without the clear identification of the *gagja*, there is no way for us to see or understand emptiness. So, therefore, **Shantideva**, in *The Bodhisattva's Way of Life*, said:

> *Without the clear identification of that of which things are empty, one cannot understand its absence, which is emptiness.*

Or, in another way,

> *Without a clear identification of the object of negation, one cannot have a clear image of emptiness.*

Shantideva was highlighting the importance of identifying the *gagja* long before seeing emptiness, through a lengthy process of analysis. Secondly, **Shantideva** said, whoever tries to understand emptiness without a clear identification of the object of negation will fall into nihilism. Why is this the case? It is because in your attempt to understand emptiness, you have to negate something. So, instead of negating the object's inherent existence, you negate the conventional existence of things and phenomena, and then you fail to posit their conventionally existent functionality. That is nihilism. **Aryadeva** said in *400 Verses*:

> *Without having a clear identification of the object of negation, whoever attempts to understand emptiness will act as a self-destroyer.*

If you fall into nihilism, you will destroy your morality. You will destroy your relations with the conventional world. **Aryadeva** also said:

> *Without having the experience and the skillful means needed to catch a poisonous snake, whoever attempts to catch that poisonous snake will be bitten.*

CRITICAL POINT TWO: THE OBJECT OF NEGATION

You must have the proper understanding and experience, and you must have the proper skill. If you do not have these but try to catch a poisonous snake, you will be bitten and destroyed. Similarly, without having a clear identification of the object of negation, whoever tries to understand emptiness will act as a self-destroyer. Therefore, it is extremely important for us to put effort into learning the ways and means to identify the object of negation before trying to identify emptiness, through the process of analysis.

There are many different ways of expressing *gagja* in the *Madhyamika* school. It is expressed as inherent existence or intrinsic existence, existing on its own side, absolutely, ultimately or truly existing, self-characterizing existence, or substantial existence.

In the *Madhyamika-Prasangika* school, these five are synonymous, that is, they have the same meaning. They are interchangeable. In the lower schools—the *Madhyamika-Svatantrika*, the *Chittamatra* and the *Vaibashika* schools—these five are not synonymous. Here, we are mainly talking about the *Madhyamika-Prasangika* school's propositions, and we will be using those five as synonymous according to our school's philosophical tradition.

The meaning of all these five is **the capability of something to exist for example as a cup, table, chair and so forth, without relying or depending on something other than itself.** If anything is fully capable to exist as a cup, say, without depending on causes and conditions, without depending on parts and fractions, and without depending upon a name, term and conceptual designation, then such a thing is identified as inherently existent. This is what inherent existence means, and that is what all those expressions mean.

According to the *Madhyamika-Prasangika* school, nothing is qualified to exist intrinsically. Nothing can be found as intrinsically existent, with inherent existence. Why? Because (as we learned earlier when studying interdependent arising) all things and phenomena arise only in dependence upon something else. All things come into being due to causes and conditions, parts and fractions, and name, term and conceptual designation, and, other than that, there is no way for anything to exist. There is no room and no way for anything to exist on its own. Something arising only in dependence upon something other than itself and something that is capable to exist without needing to depend on something other than itself are contradictory. Dependent existence and independent existence are mutually exclusive by nature. They are dichotomous, just as impermanence and permanence are dichotomous, as we discussed before.

Therefore, in the section on emptiness in the *Lamrim Chenmo* **Lama Tsongkhapa** said:

> *One is able to identify the object of negation through clearly seeing that the way things appear to our mind is in contradiction to the way things are coming into being.*

The way things are coming into being is solely through depending on something else, and nothing has the self-power to arise on its own as a cup, as a table, as a chair, etc. However, things appear to our mind as capable to exist through their own force, without need to rely on something other than themselves. Things and phenomena appear to our ordinary perception as being complete in and of themselves as, for example, a cup. This is how all things and phenomena appear to our mind. This appearance completely contradicts the actual mode of how things are coming into being.

When we recognize with the help of the five questions how things appear to our naive and un-analyzing mind, we come to the conclusion that things do appear to our mind as being inherently existent, and then we see that the naive mind unquestioningly clings to that **inherent-ness** as the mode of their existence. This very inherent existence as the apprehended object of the naive clinging mind is the object of negation or *gagja*. That inherent existence as the apprehended object of the naive clinging mind has never existed as part of what the object, for example a cup, really is, yet it simply appears. A naive mind always misapprehends things and phenomena, perceiving them in a different way than they actually exist, like a thirsty person seeing water when a mirage appears.

The easiest way to explain the object of negation is by saying it is the object of a mind that is completely mistaken with regard to the mode of existence of the apprehended object, of what it sees. The object of negation is the primary apprehended object of a mind that is grasping at self and phenomena as inherently existent. It is the primary apprehended object of an ignorant mind. This is very easy to say, but it will not help you much.

If the primary apprehended object of the mind is clock, is that primary apprehended object of that mind inherently existing clock or not? Which means, when you apprehend some object which you label clock, do you apprehend that object as a basis for it to be named a clock, as a basis of designation that can receive the name clock, or do you see it as being a clock already? Right now, we see it as being a clock already. Is the mode of seeing this object as a clock already the same as seeing it as an inherently existing clock? Yes, it is. The reason I am trying to open up many layers is to help you find the way you naturally and habitually perceive the apprehended object and then to see that this habitual way of perceiving inherent existence is to be identified as the object of negation, the *gagja*.

Clinging to Inherentness

As I said in the beginning, we see this object clock as being inherently existent, and then our naive mind unquestioningly clings to that inherent-ness as the mode of existence of the clock. The mind clings to this imagined inherent-ness as the natural basis for the object to be a clock without the aid or the interference of subjective designation. Wherever the mind clings, that is the *gagja*, the object of negation, because that imagined inherent-ness has never existed. It has never been there, and yet it always seems to appear and fool us.

That very inherent-ness that always seems to be the mode of the existence of all things is the object of negation, the *gagja*. That is the one to which the naive mind always clings. The mind itself that clings to that inherent-ness is not the object of negation. The cup or whatever, the thing named, is not the object of negation. The object of negation is the inherent-ness which seems to be the mode of existence of the cup and indeed of all things and phenomena. That is the specific object to be refuted and negated; it has never existed as part of the named object and has never existed as the mode of being of that object. It is a one hundred percent false appearance that has nothing to do with the true nature of the object's reality. It has nothing to do with what the object really is and how the object really exists. The appearance of a mirage being water is one hundred percent false. Likewise, the appearance of all things and phenomena being inherently existent in or under their own power is one hundred percent false.

False Appearance

Normally, as we have said, things appear to our mind as being inherently existent. The inherent-ness of any object always comes to our mind or perception as its actual mode of existence. The naive mind always assents, believes or clings to that appearance as the way things actually exist. To repeat—Belief in that very inherent-ness as the mode of existence is the *gagja*, the object of negation.

The mind that always clings to inherent-ness as being the mode of existence of all things and phenomena is completely faulty and deluded. To repeat—That inherent-ness which seems to be the mode of being of all things and phenomena has never been existent, but it always appears to our dualistic mind. The appearance of inherent existence as the mode of existence of all things and phenomena is the object of negation. And again, that appearance is one hundred percent false and illusory. That appearance has no truth in relation to the very fact of how things actually exist.

Remember that inherent existence means the existence of anything, for example a cup, solely at its very substantial level, without the need of a designating term that is to be imputed by a conventional mind. Inherent existence would be the self-generated identity of cup-ness, the self-imposed identity of cup, the self-characterization of cup, or a self-established identity of cup. These are all slightly different ways of expressing inherent existence, but they all have the same meaning: a particular object cup that would have inherent existence would exist as a cup only in reference to itself, without relying or depending on causes and conditions, parts and fractions, names and terms, and a designator.

Such a thing has never existed, and such a thing is an impossibility. Which means we cannot find anything that exists in that manner. Existing in that manner—having inherent existence—is not the way for any thing or phenomenon to exist. However, all things and phenomena appear to our mind to be existing in that manner. Therefore, that appearance is false, illusive, and deceptive. Unless we identify that this is the way that things appear to our mind in contradiction to the way things actually exist, we cannot understand the true meaning of emptiness.

Recognizing False Appearance

So, to review once more, how does one identify from his or her own experience that the way things appear to the mind is, as **Lama Tsongkhapa** said, in contradiction to the way they are coming into being? You will understand that only when you see how what appears to your mind somehow does not really match reality. So, therefore, in the very beginning we said, there is a mismatch. There is a disparity between appearance and fact. When you see that mismatch between appearance and fact—when you see that the way things appear does not really match to the fact—then, if you put more mindful effort into observing that, it becomes clear to you that the way things appear to your mind is not the way they actually exist.

For example, the object clock appears as existing at the very substantial level, and that appearance gives you the impression that the object clock possesses a quality of clock-ness that is locatable or findable somewhere within its substantial components as the self-generated identity of clock. Regardless of whether we name it as a clock or not, we think that object exists as a clock in its very substantial base and that it exists as a clock only in reference to itself. This is the way that the clock appears to our mind. This does not match the very fact of the mode of the existence of the clock. Why does not this match? Because the closer you look, the less the clock becomes findable as a clock at its base. The more we analyze the object, the less the clock is findable. Because the closer you look, the less the clock becomes findable as a clock. The more we analyze, the less the clock is findable.

When you do not analyze it—when you are in a naive and un-analyzing state—the object appears as concrete, solid and with a self-characterized identity of clock. When you start analyzing, that identity seems to melt down and dissolve. It becomes less and less findable. We have to at least get to that point to see that the way the object appears to our mind does not match to the fact of how it actually exists. This is the only way we can see and we can know that the way all things and phenomena appear to our mind is in contradiction to the way they actually exist.

No matter how long, how far and how deeply you contemplate about the mismatch between how things appear and how they actually exist, it will not help you to understand the true meaning of emptiness until you fully negate or refute the inherent-ness of the object that seems to be the actual manner in which it is coming into being. The inherent-ness of the object which seems to be the actual mode of its coming into being is called the object to be negated in order to give rise to the image of emptiness in your mind. This explanation gives you enough information to recognize the object of negation, the *gagja*.

Critical Point Two: The Object of Negation

With this, we have completed the lengthy discussion on the object of negation and the way to identify it. We have completed the first two of the five points we listed as critical to understanding emptiness. If you have a pretty good understanding of the first critical point, interdependent origination, that understanding will lead to seeing how things falsely appear to the mind, in contradiction to the way they actually exist. This false appearance is the *gagja* or object of negation. So, following the discussion of interdependent origination, the first critical point, we have discussed the second critical point, the necessity to identify the object of negation and how to identify it. But as we have said, this understanding is still very fragile in our mind.

Now we are ready for the third critical point for understanding emptiness. This is the mere detection of the absence of the *gagja* or object of negation. Like the other critical points, it is not so easy and we will need a lot of repetition for it to sink in!

Chapter Eighteen

Critical Point Three: Mere Detection of the Absence of the Gagja

The Realization of Emptiness Arises as the Mere Detection of the Absence of the *Gagja*

THE THIRD CRITICAL POINT deals with how the realization of emptiness takes place. The first critical point, interdependent origination, leads to the second critical point, the definition of the *gagja*. In studying the second critical point we learned what the *gagja* is, what is to be negated, but the concept is still very fragile in our mind. With the third critical point we will reinforce the definition of the *gagja* and learn how to actually see emptiness. As we said, the third critical point is the mere detection of the absence of the *gagja* or object of negation. We will need to go over and over the definition of the *gagja* in the process of trying to hold it and actually see its absence. The realization of emptiness takes place as the mere detection of the absence of the *gagja* or object of negation. It is the mere detection of the lack of intrinsic existence in all things and phenomena. The moment you detect the absence of the object of negation, this is qualified to be the actual realization of emptiness. At first, this realization will be very fragile, very fleeting, very momentary.

First, as we have said, without having a clear identification of the *gagja,* the object of negation, we cannot realize emptiness at all. In studying the second critical point we have learned a bit about the *gagja*, but it is not yet very familiar. The way to become familiar with the object of negation is to pay mindful attention towards all things and phenomena in our everyday life, trying to see how things appear to our ordinary and naive mind or perception, until we start seeing some disparity between how we ordinarily perceive and how things themselves now actually can seem to have a different mode of existence, so that we have less tendency simply to rely on first appearance. We learn not to consent to the appearance, and we have less trust in the ordinary appearance. We are motivated to look behind and beyond the ordinary appearance, through the analytic process.

Second, once we have a clear idea of how things normally appear to our mind, then we should carry out some experiment or analysis to see whether or not things really exist the way they appear to our mind. Based on your own experience and analysis, you must become convinced that the way things appear to your naive mind does not match the way things actually exist. If things would exist in the way they appear, then things and phenomena should have self-generated or self-powered existence that is not the result of causes and conditions, that is not subject to causes and conditions, that cannot interact with other phenomena, and that should not have a different appearance from the viewpoint of different perceivers.

Critical Point Three: Mere Detection of the Absence of the *Gagja*

When we carefully consider the two steps described earlier—that is, when we carefully go through the two step process of first identifying the object of negation and then analyzing how we habitually see things in contrast to what is the true mode of existence of things and phenomena—we will get some kind of hint as to the mismatch between the way things appear to our mind and the way things actually exist. Even though we will not yet have a full understanding of the way things actually exist, we can still gain some clue or hint that there is a mismatch between the way things exist and how things appear. So, this is how we can approach an understanding of emptiness, by going through those two sequential steps.

The Meaning of *Gagja*: Five Questions

Earlier we asked ourselves five questions about how objects appear to us, so that we could get an idea of what exactly is the *gagja*, what exactly needs to be refuted. Now that we understand what the *gagja* is, we will consider five more, somewhat related, questions. These five new questions lead to the deep meaning of the *gagja*, and from there to a better understanding of the actual mode of existence of all objects. In brief, we have said that the meaning of the *gagja* or object of negation is the quality of inherent-ness that we tend to see in all things. Remember that the object of negation is definitely not the specific thing that is the object of the mind at the moment, but rather it is something we perceive in everything we see, namely a self-powered or self-generated identity arising solely from the side of the object. We tend to assume this self-power in everything we perceive. We assume there is some self-generated identity that really exists at the very fundamental level.

The five questions which you need to raise in your mind and which you need to carefully consider in order to crystallize the deep meaning of the object of negation, what the object of negation means, are:

- First, if things have a self-generated identity or self-powered identity, then why do they depend on causes and conditions, and why do things not come into being under their own power rather than through causes and conditions?
- The second question is, if things have a self-powered identity of cup-ness or table-ness, for example, then why do they need parts and fractions that compose the whole?
- Third, if things have a self-generated identity, then why cannot that self-generated identity be found within the material parts, components or constituents?
- Fourth, if things have a self-powered identity of cup or chair, so and so forth, then why do they change appearance from the viewpoint of the different perceivers?
- And finally, if things have a self-generated identity from their own side, then why do they require to be named as a cup, as a chair and so forth?

After carefully considering these five questions, you will become convinced that no thing or phenomenon has any self-generated identity that makes the object what it is, without the need of the conventional designating term. For example, for any particular room to exist as an office room, it requires someone to designate it as such. Being labeled is the only way through which that room can exist as an office, a bedroom, so and so forth. Other than that, that particular room itself does not have the self-characterization of office-room-ness. So, we need to consider those five questions. Those are all natural questions that you would ask in your analysis. They all require an answer, if you are going to say things are inherently existent.

If anything would have the self-power to exist under its own choice, under its own right, without need to rely on something other than itself—whether it be causes and conditions, parts and fractions, or conceptual designation—then, that would be an intrinsically existent thing. Things really do not exist in that manner, but we perceive them that way. To see the difference between that imagined intrinsic existence and the way things actually exist is the purpose of identifying the object of negation, as we have explained in the second critical point.

That **intrinsic-ness** or inherent-ness has never existed. However, as we know, things always appear to our mind to exist in that way, and we always assent to that appearance believing that this is the way things exist. Accordingly, we react or respond to things as they appear, which contradicts how they exist. Our mind is deeply confused between how things appear and how things actually exist, and this serves as the primary source for all types of mental, emotional and psychological pain and suffering. Once you understand that, then inherent existence, intrinsic existence, true existence, ultimate existence, absolute existence and objective existence are synonymous.

We have said that inherently existent means a quality of something that has the self-power to exist under its own right without need to rely on something other than itself. That is the meaning of inherent existence, that is what we call the object of negation, and that is the one thing that needs to be refuted. That needs to be dismantled in order to see how things really are. Dismantling the object of negation is the way to penetrate into the very true nature of reality that lies beyond false appearance.

Once we know how to identify the object of negation and have in mind a clear identification of the object of negation, we need to go through logical analysis in order to ascertain emptiness by refuting the presence of what we always assumed was there.

Two Types of Analysis in the Search for Emptiness

There are two types of analysis we can use in the search for the emptiness of all things and phenomena: first, the analysis of searching for the imputed or designated term which seems to pervade the entirety of the object, and second, the analysis of deconstructing the material parts from the gross level down to subatomic particles.

First Type of Analysis: Imputation

From the first type of analysis we learn how we impute an identity or a term upon the object and then instantly fail to recognize that the term is merely an imputation that is neither part of the object nor in any way connected to the object. Finding the process of imputation leads us to identify the object of negation. We have already gone over much of this, but it is worthwhile to repeat! There is an existing thing in front of you which is a base, a basis of imputation, and there is something that your mind imputes upon that object which is a designation. So, if you can distinguish between what is the base, which is a set of characteristics yet to be named, and what name you impute upon it for your conventional needs, then you can clearly see the distinction between what the mind creates through imputation and what is actually there.

So, now you have recognized the object of negation. You know what the mind imputes, where the mind imputes, and why the mind imputes, and, through the process of negating the object's intrinsic existence that you previously thought to be the mode of the existence of all things, you at last find the emptiness of the object. You have accomplished the third critical point, which is detecting the absence of the *gagja*, but this moment is fleeting. Therefore we will go over the process again, and go a little deeper.

Conventional terms—such as, cup, table, chair, John, Katie and so forth—pop up in our mind when we see anything. We have the intention to employ the term, to apply that term to a certain thing, in order for that thing to exist as a cup, as a chair and so forth with a conventional function to fulfill our needs. In this process of imputation, we fail to recognize that we are giving a name to the object, that we are merely designating it as such and such. Therefore, we see the imputed name as being the same as the object to which it is applied, and this way of seeing gives us a belief that all things are intrinsically or inherently existent—existent through their own nature. Whatever term we designate on the object it appears to us as built within the object, and we never consider that the term comes from our own mind and not through the object's intrinsic force. This is why we must be able to distinguish the name from the object which is serving as a base for that imputed name. By doing that, you can clearly distinguish what you have imputed upon that valid base and what needs to be negated in order to cognize that object's emptiness, its ultimate mode of being.

This first type of analysis involves searching within the object for the designated term that always seems to be intrinsically part of the object. We come to see that there are two separate things, the designating term and what the term is designated upon. And as we know by now, what the term is designated upon is called the basis imputation or basis of designation.

Three Factors of Designation

When talking about designation, we say there are three necessary factors of designation, as when the term clock is set up by conceptualization. The three factors are first, a designator—the person with his conceptual mind. The second thing needed is a term to be designated upon something, in this case "clock." Finally there is that object upon which the term is applied, that object we call the basis of designation. The basis of designation is a set of interdependently arisen characteristics such as color, shape, texture, taste, smell and so forth which is yet to be named.

In our example, the term is clock. Clock is a term or designation which is set up by conceptualization. Also, there is a funny looking thing which is a set of characteristics having color, shape, size, texture and so forth, and which is yet to be named. If we assume that before we designate the term clock onto that phenomenon it should exist as a clock already, then we believe that the object exists inherently as a clock without depending on the name for it to exist as a clock. We have this naive assumption or feeling that the object clock should have something within its substantial constituents which makes it a clock long before we name it as a clock.

Currently, we see everything as inherently real, and, when we do not see things as inherently real, we undermine their existence. We undermine their existence by thinking they are unworthy to have, or are useless or meaningless. We deny or disqualify their conventional validity. We reject their conventional existence, and so we are inclined towards nihilism. How to posit conventional reality is the fourth critical point and we will discuss it fully later on.

Continuing with this third critical point, detecting the *gagja*, there is a designating term and there is something upon which that term is designated, a set of characteristics which is yet to be named as a clock. Before we name or label those characteristics as a clock, there is no clock that exists within its parts. First, you have to establish that there is no characteristic within that set of characteristics which actually qualifies as a clock. You have to establish clearly that there cannot be anything within those parts that makes it a clock. Otherwise, that is, if you could find clock-ness, there would be no reason to name it as a clock; it would be a clock already.

Valid Basis of Imputation

Unless we have a clear understanding of what qualifies something to be the basis of imputation for the term clock, we might ask, "Why don't we impute the term clock onto just anything? Why only on this particular set of characteristics? Is there really any difference between a valid basis and any other basis?" Like rejecting conventional reality, not recognizing a difference between valid and invalid also could lead to nihilism: "Anything can be a clock or nothing can be clock, so who cares? I do not care! Let's go get drunk." If we are mulling over these kinds of questions, it shows we do not understand the purpose of

Critical Point Three: Mere Detection of the Absence of the Gagja

imputation and the mode of imputation. We do not yet have a clear understanding of what qualifies something to be a valid basis for a specific concordant term. Because of this reason, once we get to the point where we can separate the term from the object, we might think that anything can be a clock or nothing can be a clock. But here we have to realize that what qualifies something to be a valid basis for a specific term is not some inherently existent set of characteristics, but that the basis perfectly matches and can perfectly perform the function that we assign to it by giving it that name. This is a terribly important point, and bears repeating—What qualifies something to be a valid basis for a specific term is not some inherently existent set of characteristics, but that the basis perfectly matches and can perfectly perform the function that we assign to it by giving it that name.

So, again, we can see that there are the three necessary things, namely our self as designator, a designated term and a basis of designation. Clock exists as the result of the mere process of imputation onto a base, a basis of designation. The problem, as we have said, is that when we designate a term upon something the term somehow pervades or infuses the entirety of the object. The term pervades and concretizes all over the constituents, with the result that the entire object appears to be identical with the term.

Instead of knowing the term to be a term that is imputed by our mind, we see the object as possessing a self-generated identity of cup, for example. This happens because it never occurs to us that the term was something we applied. The wholeness of the constituents of the cup appears to our mind to be the term cup, which is very convincing. We believe that this is the way cup exists. It is very difficult to separate and to get into the habit of separating, the term from the object and the object from the term.

This first type of analysis—analysis of imputation— involves searching to see if the designated term really exists as part of the object or not, in other words, searching within the object for the designated term that always seems to be intrinsically part of the object. When we are seeking in this way, from time to time we will get a glimpse of experience that the term is not one with the base. At the same time, that glimpse of experience is easily disturbed by the arising of the feeling or thought of, "How could this be?" The belief or assumption that objects are the same as their name is so ingrained in us that it is almost impossible to maintain that glimpse without it being destroyed by the feeling that things simply cannot exist that way, that really objects and their names are the same.

Second Type of Analysis: Material Deconstruction

As we said earlier, there are two types of analysis here, the analysis of imputation and the analysis of material deconstruction. The two types of analysis will not be effective for causing you to cognize emptiness unless you have mastered the second critical point and have in mind the clear identification of the object of negation. Remember that the *gagja*, or object of negation, is that inherent-ness of the object which seems to be the actual mode of its coming into being. The way to perform those two types of analysis in order to establish the emptiness of any object is by making sure that your identification of the object of negation remains clear and active in your mind and then applying one of those two types of analysis in order to detect the emptiness of any object.

We have already discussed the first type of analysis, the analysis of imputation. The second type of analysis involves disassembling or deconstructing the components of the object from its grossest level to the most subtle subatomic particles until you get to the point where the components—the particles—are so small, so tiny or so subtle that they are indivisible into smaller component particles.

When you disassemble or deconstruct the parts of the object you will not find what you always assumed was present within the object or what you always thought the object was. What we always assumed

CRITICAL POINT THREE: MERE DETECTION OF THE ABSENCE OF THE *GAGJA*

was there is some substantial thing that can be found as the identity of that object. For example, a cup: We feel that there must be or should be a substantial material identity or material thing, that makes the object what it is, a cup. There must be some substantial thing within the object that justifies it to exist as cup and demands that it exist as and be named a cup.

Before now, we have always assumed the presence of an inherently substantial entity qualified to be the cup; we have always assumed that this entity existed somewhere within its component parts, inherently. That is what we assumed makes the object exist as a cup, as a table, so and so forth. Trying to prove our assumption, we look for and we expect to find some substantial thing that qualifies it to be a cup in and of itself, that demands that it be a cup. But now you have deconstructed the material components from the grossest level way down to the subatomic particles, and you have not found something that you always assumed to be there.

When you do not find anything at its very substantial level that qualifies it to exist as cup in and of itself, then not finding what you always believed to be there—namely, the very thing which makes the object what you have named it, such as a cup—in that very moment, you lose the appearance of the cup. In that very moment, you lose the sense of that being a cup, and you fail to posit the existence of the cup. At this point, there are three conclusive possibilities, namely that the object no longer appears to your mind as a cup, and therefore, you lose the appearance of the cup. Or, you lose the sense of that object being a cup. The third possibility is that you completely fail to posit that being a cup.

This is where you have truly arrived at the third critical point, the mere detection of the absence of the *gagja*. Even though you might have lost the cup, just meditate now on this **vacuity**, even though you feel quite uncomfortable seeing nothing where before you saw a cup.

Stabilizing Freshly Experienced Emptiness

Meditation is a tool for stabilizing the freshly experienced emptiness of the cup. The meditating mind performs the process of analysis which involves first examining imputation and then deconstructing the components with the hope of finding something that you always thought to be there and to make the object what it really is. Not finding what you expected, you have a sense of vacuity, of absence. Then that very meditating mind must remain with the mere experience of vacuity without anything to grasp onto. It remains in the mere experience of the absence of what you always believed to be there. At this point, simply ignore that as soon as the cup lost its seemingly solid appearance it disappeared. Concentrate now on the new experience of vacuity—the lack of inherent existence of the cup.

The first moment of the mere vacuity can be very striking to your mind. That very first moment of the experience of emptiness is followed by the emotional feeling of fear, a sense of loss and a sense of being alone or lonely. This will definitely cause you to retreat, to pull back or step back from that experience and immediately return to a non-meditating mind. Because you are very new to that experience and that experience is completely unfamiliar, novel and contradictory to what you always expected, you immediately return to your normal way of seeing and experiencing which gives you a sense of comfort and security: "Oh good, things are normal again."

The tendency always to retreat or pull back the moment we have that experience of vacuity is extremely difficult to overcome. It requires a strong familiarity with the experience of vacuity that we will only gain through repeated meditation employing analysis and concentration. Analysis will allow us to strengthen or regain that powerful experience, and then we simply abide or rest in that experience through concentration, without doing further analysis.

In the beginning, as you repeatedly practice meditating on the vacuity, you will find that gradually, gradually, after you have been

CRITICAL POINT THREE: MERE DETECTION OF THE ABSENCE OF THE GAGJA

abiding or resting in that experience for a certain period of time, the very strength or force of that vacuity will degrade or diminish. It will become more and more shallow. Through repeating the analytic process, you can regain the full force of that experience before again resting on it through concentration. Through that repeated process of analysis as the means to regain the experience of vacuity and then resting on it to become more familiar with that experience, we can make ourselves fully familiar with that experience of vacuity. After some time, that experience no longer generates emotional disturbances such as fear, loneliness, a sense of loss, and so forth, and it becomes easier and easier to remain concentrated on that experience of vacuity in meditation with a sense of joy and comfort.

If we do not have the clear identification of the object of negation, simply deconstructing or disassembling the components of the object only serves to destroy conventional reality. We may be inclined to say, "Cup does not exist. This does not exist, and that does not exist." This is nihilism and not emptiness, so that is an extremely important thing to bear in mind.

Some teachers teach emptiness the very easy way, saying, "If you realize that a book has a hundred pages, then you just keep going through these pages, saying page number one is not the book, page number two is not the book, page number ninety-nine is not the book, page number one hundred is not the book. If you realize each page of the book is not the book, then you have realized emptiness." However, this is not the meaning of emptiness, at all. Simply not finding what you are looking for in itself is not realizing emptiness. Simply not finding what you are looking for is not the same as finding the nonexistence of what you are looking for. That is the powerful *Madhyamika* school lawyer's defense of its own system. In the *Uma gongpa rabsel, Clear Exposition on Emptiness,* **Lama Tsongkhapa** says:

> *Simply not finding the one that you are looking for is not the same as finding the nonexistence of what you are looking for.*

If you really find the nonexistence of what you are looking for instead of simply not finding what you are looking for, you will see that there is a difference and you will see the difference. So, simply not finding what you are looking for is alone not the meaning of realizing emptiness. The meaning of realizing emptiness is the finding of the nonexistence of what you are looking for, in other words, detecting the nonexistence or absence of the *gagja*.

When you find the nonexistence of what you are looking for, that nonexistence will not dismantle the conventional existence of the cup, for example. The cup does exist, but it does not exist with the self-characterization of cup-ness which we had naively assumed was there. Finding the nonexistence of what you are looking for—in this case, finding the nonexistence of a self-characterization of cup-ness—will keep the conventional reality of the cup intact. Soon we will examine this more fully when we discuss the fourth critical point.

Interdependent Arising Confirms Emptiness

In the beginning of this discussion of the third critical point, we said the realization of emptiness occurs or arises as the mere detection of the absence of inherent existence, no more than that, no less than that. In all of the *Madhyamika* philosophical teachings, you will find that interdependent arising is the most obvious evidence that all things are empty of independent existence, inherent existence, intrinsic existence and self-characterization, that because of interdependent arising nothing is a self-powered entity or a self-generated entity. Therefore, the dependent arising and interdependent existence of anything must confirm that thing as being empty of inherent existence. In the same way, something being honey confirms it as being sweet. Do we think it is sour? Or, does the fact that it is honey decisively, unmistakenly confirm it as being sweet? Similar to this, that anything has dependent existence must confirm that that thing is empty of inherent existence. Therefore, interdependent arising confirms emptiness.

CRITICAL POINT THREE: MERE DETECTION OF THE ABSENCE OF THE GAGJA

As we have discussed, the most prominent, leading philosophers of the *Madhyamika* school—**Nagarjuna, Aryadeva, Chandrakirti, Buddhapalita, Lama Tsongkhapa**—unanimously agree that emptiness must be understood within the context of interdependent origination. *Pratītyasamutpāda*, in Sanskrit, means dependent arising, interdependent origination, interdependent arising, or interdependent coexistence. As we said before when discussing the first critical point, the meaning of dependent arising is not limited only to things arising from causes and conditions but must be understood as obviating any self-power in all things and phenomena. Things have no inherent existence or self-power to exist through their own choice, under their own right, or through their own nature, and emptiness must be understood within the context of dependent arising.

The complete meaning of interdependent arising must be understood as a mere lack of self-power in all things and phenomena to exist through their own choice, under their own right, or through their own nature, and emptiness must be understood within the context of dependent arising because the meaning of dependent arising is the mere lack of self-power in all things and phenomena to exist through their own nature.

As we know, all things and phenomena arise interdependently. Therefore they have no inherent existence, despite their false appearance to our deluded mind. The consequence of interdependent arising is that nothing has self-power. That is why emptiness must be understood within the context of dependent arising, because the deep consequence of dependent arising is the mere lack of self-power in all things and phenomena to exist through their own nature.

Once we understand that, then we can see that dependent arising and emptiness are two different aspects of the same phenomenon or two different perspectives on the same thing. Once we understand that, then we can see that dependent arising and emptiness are complementary and not contradictory.

Interdependent Arising, Emptiness, Appearance, and Function

At this point, we can begin to link interdependent arising and emptiness with appearance and function. The **Panchen Lama Lobsang Chökyi Gyaltsen,** who lived from 1570 until 1662, wrote in his *Lama Chopa* or *Guru Puja* that

> *The realization of emptiness is complete once you see that all things lack inherent existence and yet still appear and function like a mirage, a dream, a magical emanation, a rainbow, and a reflection on a clear lake.*

In the case of the mirage, there is an appearance which we call a mirage. It has the appearance of existing substantially, but when we analyze, examine or get closer to it—no matter what method we use to locate it—there is nothing there which is findable. There is only vacuity. So just as water is unfindable where the mirage is, nothing is findable to exist inherently within the parts or whole of the mirage. Which means, the closer we look, the less solid it becomes and, in the end, there is nothing left but the mere appearance. Dreams are similar to this. Also, during a magic act, we are entertained by the magician's creations, but there is nothing to grasp onto. There is nothing to justify our attachment to those magical emanations, because they are just mere appearance.

Reflections also appear real and can deceive. For example, a proud dog who is holding a piece of meat in his mouth walks with the pride of having found that meat and of carrying that meat. While crossing a bridge he looks into the water and sees his own reflection. Seeing another proud figure, he barks to scare it away and drops the meat into the lake. Why did he lose the meat? He was deceived by the mere appearance of his own reflection which be believed was another

Critical Point Three: Mere Detection of the Absence of the Gagja

real dog that might try to take his meat. Like that, reflections appear real to us.

Lama Tsongkhapa, in his very short and dense *Lam-tso Nam-sum* or *Three Principal Aspects of the Path*, says:

> *Your realization of emptiness is complete when you know all things lack intrinsic existence while cause and effect and dependent arising are unfailing.*

The function of cause and effect is unfailing and yet the cause and effect themselves are empty of inherent existence. When you see these two—emptiness and interdependent arising—as complementary and not contradictory, then your realization of emptiness is complete and fully mature. This only happens after long study, contemplation and meditation as well as frequent and repeated analysis.

Lama Tsongkhapa also says:

> *Your realization of emptiness is complete when you lose your sense of the inherent existence of things and phenomena merely upon seeing them as being dependently arising.*

Which means, merely seeing things and phenomena as being dependently arisen must cause you to lose your sense of them as being inherently existent. When you detect the absence of the *gagja* by seeing all things as interdependently arisen and therefore not inherently existent you have realized emptiness. Things no longer seem to be inherently solid, or something to grasp upon or attach to. Once that happens delusive thoughts and emotions can no longer arise and influence our actions and deeds.

After familiarity with the fact that emptiness and interdependent arising do not contradict—which you gain through repeated meditation—you are ready for the fourth critical point, how to posit conventional reality although all things are empty of inherent existence.

Chapter Nineteen

Critical Point Four: How to Posit Conventional Reality

Intellectual Understanding

THROUGH STUDYING AND LEARNING, we gain some intellectual understanding of emptiness, but still we will have an internal conflict between how things appear to our mind and what we now intellectually know about their true nature. For a long time, we will be unable to reconcile those two. Frequently, the questions will arise: "How can things function if they are empty? How can things be empty if they are functional?" Until this conflict is completely resolved, our realization of emptiness cannot be perfected.

Functionality

So far, we have discussed in depth the first three critical points in understanding emptiness, namely interdependent arising, the *gagja* or object of negation, and realizing emptiness by merely detecting the *gagja*.

Now we come to the fourth critical point, which is how to posit conventional reality and functionality although all things are empty of inherent existence. We say, "although," but this shows our confusion, because the first thing we must realize, if we think about it, is that things do not function in spite of being empty of inherent existence but rather things function just because they are empty.

Once you have some acceptance of the fact that things are empty of intrinsic existence, due to interdependent arising, there is a tendency to try figure out how things can function despite being empty. Contrary to what you might first think, as we said, their functionality is actually dependent upon their being empty, upon being interdependent, because, as we said before, the impermanent, ever changing nature of things allows interaction among them. **Lama Tsongkhapa** is saying the same thing in a different way when he says that your realization of emptiness is complete when you can see all things and phenomena as capable to function and being empty at the same time. When **Lama Tsongkhapa** says that your realization of emptiness is complete when you can see all things and phenomena as able to function and being empty at the same time, he is pointing to the intimate relationship between emptiness and functionality. As we now know, emptiness comes from the universal interdependence of all things and phenomena.

Remember that **Lama Tsongkhapa** also said:

> *When we see emptiness in terms of the meaning of dependent origination, then being empty of inherent existence and capable to function do not contradict.*

As we said, things function because they are empty. A thing is not disqualified from being functional because it is dependently arisen and thus empty of inherent existence. Rather, its functionality depends on its very changeableness, a quality it gets from being interdependently arisen. It is this changeableness that allows it to interact with other, changeable, phenomena. This is a deep and important point!

Lama Tsongkhapa is saying that you lose your sense of things as being inherently real and thus something to grasp onto merely by seeing them as dependently arisen, which confirms that emptiness and dependent arising must be complementary. Your realization of emptiness is not complete if you still see emptiness and dependent arising as two distinct and unrelated phenomena so that when you see things as dependently arisen, you do not see them as empty, or when you see things as empty, you do not at the same time see them as dependently arisen. If you do not see these two qualities simultaneously your realization of emptiness is incomplete. But even when you have seen emptiness and know it is the natural, unique by-product of interdependent arising, when you can see them both at the same time, as we have said, for some time you have trouble viewing the object as capable to function when you see it as empty of inherent existence. The object disappears altogether when you momentarily realize its emptiness. There are two points: 1) emptiness is the natural by-product of interdependent arising; 2) functionality is possible just because of emptiness/interdependent arising.

Positing Conventional Reality

When we train to see that things do not have intrinsic existence and we are able to negate false appearance, as we have just said we might still have trouble seeing the conventional reality that lies behind the appearance. A thing appears. Until we train, the object that appears seems substantially real. When we analyze and find the absence of the *gagja* we recognize that the appearance of being intrinsically real is false. Then we ask, "If this appearance is false, how can I still see things, how can things still appear but no longer have that false appearance of inherent existence? Also, if things are empty of inherent existence, how can we posit their functionality or conventional validity? If all things and phenomena are empty, do they even really exist? If things are empty of inherent or substantial existence—if things do not have any form of self-characterization or self-evidence—then do they really exist?" These questions, like those asking how things can be empty and still function, or be functional but empty lead to the fourth critical point, which is how to posit the conventional reality.

We ask, "If things are empty, how do we establish or posit their conventional existence, their functionality?" Things and phenomena do exist but they do not exist in the way we normally think they do. We have covered that in the detailed discussion of the second and the third critical points. Now we need to learn to see the conventional, functional appearance while we no longer believe in the false appearance of inherent existence.

Conventional Appearance and Conceptual Designation

Recall that in the *Madhyamika* school—particularly *Prasangika-Madhyamika*—things exist only at the level of mere conceptual designation. Which means, as we have said, things do not possess a self-identity of what they are, such as snake, rope, cup, table, chair, books, pens, so and so forth. Things do not possess self-generated identity, but things do have an identity of what they are in dependence upon conceptual designation. Which means, a conceptual mind designates, applies, gives or provides a certain term or characterization to the object, and it is that term which permits the object's base to appear as that particular phenomenon to that conventional designating mind. The way things actually exist is as designated objects which lie within the level of mere appearance. We understand by now that our designation is only a name and that it does not give any **intrinsic reality** to the object. The object exists only at the level of **mere appearance** and thus offers nothing to grasp onto.

At this point we need to understand something very important about appearance, what **appearance** means. As we have said, the appearance of the designated object is initially or originally based merely upon a process of characterization given by a conventional conceptual mind. You see an object and give it a name based on your subjective experience of it.

We say the object's appearance is initially or originally based merely upon a process of characterization given by a conceptual mind. **Initially** or **originally** means right from the beginning the base, the object, the basis of designation, does not have the self-characterization to be what we name it. The way the object comes into existence as cup, chair, table, etc. is by being named. This statement is not implying that later on the object acquires some kind of self-existence. By initially we mean that at first an object has no characterization—it is just a collection of parts that is yet to be named—but it comes into existence as such and such solely by being named. This is the way an object comes into existence with a conventionally agreed upon function—only through the process of conceptual designation.

From the very beginning, the object itself lacks any form of self-identity. The way the object comes into being—right from the beginning—as a cup, table, so and so forth, is through the process of conceptual designation. In the beginning, how it comes into being is through the process of characterization that is given by the conventional subjective mind. This point cannot be stressed too often, because it is so very important!

First, how do you feel about this? Do you feel comfortable with things existing only at the level of mere appearance based on the characterization given by our own conventional subjective mind? At the beginning everybody will feel uncomfortable with the idea that things exist only at the level of mere appearance because we all assume that things exist solidly on their own side. It is necessary to familiarize yourself with the new way of thinking instead of always seeking the comfort of what is unrealistic but already familiar. This is all about training—analyzing carefully and meditating on the result of the analysis.

Secondly, if things really do exist only at the level of mere appearance, then can things really perform a function? How do we establish conventional reality or existence? Can we understand that things exist only at the level of mere appearance but at the same time have the functional capability to fulfill our conventional needs based on the term and characterization that are given by our own conventional subjective mind, and not based upon things having a self-characterizing essence? Remember here that things function because of their interdependent existence, their emptiness, not in spite of it. We need to keep this fact well in mind.

In front of us there is something that is not yet named, and therefore that does not exist as a particular object with a particular function—for instance a cup, table, chair, so and so forth. If you think that it exists as something, then it already exists as something as the result of your designation, not from its own power or through its own nature. You call it a something; it is "a something." It is a thing. You just named it a thing. So, your mind—with or without reason—has characterized it to be something. That is all.

For example, take an object you name "clock." After you name it, it exists as a clock only at the level of mere appearance based on the characterization that has been set up by the mind and imputed upon that object. Through this process, the consensual reality of that object as a clock appears and is conventionally agreed upon without room or need to disagree with regard to its function. This is how conventional reality comes into being.

Appearance and Aspect or Reflection

It is important to understand the meaning of the word appearance in this context. Appearance is not the same as the concept or idea of any phenomenon, for instance, a clock. An object appears to your mind and causes you to say, "I see a clock." So appearance of the clock means, one that serves for your individual, subjective consciousness to arise with that reflection, or as **Dharmakirti** says, "in that aspect." To put it another way, appearance means one that causes your mind to arise with that content. The easiest way to say this is that appearance means the object's mere reflection causes the mind to arise in that aspect.

Reflection means that once we assign a term such as cup or clock to an object, then whenever we see the object the term cup reflects out of this object and our mind automatically makes a link between the term and the object—but the term cannot be found in the object, neither separate or as one with the object. Since we are automatically able to make the link, the object is capable to fulfill our needs in the way we initially assigned that name, not randomly, but solely for our conventional needs and necessity.

In the text, it says, "in that aspect." An **aspect** is an object's appearance when perceived from a certain viewpoint. From your point of view, something appears as attractive. However, the same object might appear as unattractive from someone else's viewpoint. One object can have different aspects in relation to different perceivers or perceiving minds. So, appearance means the mere reflection of the object that causes your individual mind to arise in that aspect, perhaps in a slightly different way from other individual perceivers, depending on their different karmic tendencies. This explains why there can be disagreement about the characteristics of any object.

Returning to the example, an object that you could name clock appears to your sense consciousness. Your sense consciousness manifests in that aspect, and you name it a clock.

Positing Conventional Reality Alongside Emptiness

So, appearance means a reflection of the object that fundamentally causes our individual consciousness to arise in that aspect. The way things actually exist is only at the level of mere appearance to a perceiving mind. All things are interdependently arisen, interdependent, and thus empty. Apart from that, things do not have a different mode in which they come into being with conventionally identifiable or recognizable characterization. At this point you might despair and ask, "So, how can we possibly posit conventional reality alongside emptiness?" **Lama Tsongkhapa** understood this difficulty well and he said:

The process of positing conventional reality is more subtle than establishing the emptiness of all things.

Positing, establishing or realizing emptiness is easier than positing conventional reality alongside emptiness. This idea can be disturbing until we carefully examine. We understand that emptiness means the absence of inherent existence in all things because they are interdependently arisen. Things have no intrinsic existence and therefore they are empty and exist solely by being named from a subjective standpoint by an individual conceptual mind. Conventional reality means that all the things named are functional and are capable to function in the way they are named—when they are named accurately.

In brief, the way conventional reality exists is neither more than a designated name nor not merely a designated name. If things exist as a mere designated name, then this disqualifies their functionality. If things are more than a designated name, then this implies inherent characterization. Conventional reality exists as a mere reference to the name that is given to an object when the appearance of the object causes the designating mind to arise in that aspect. For example, such an object called clock exists as a mere reference to the name clock that is applied to a valid base.

Nothing Exists at the Material Level

As we know, when we analyze or search for the very mode of existence of things and phenomena with the hope of finding what they really are—a cup, a table, a chair, and so forth—or with the hope of finding their existence at the material level, we cannot find what they are or find them at all at the substantial level. If we carefully analyze their very existence with the hope of finding their essence at the material level beyond their appearance, then we cannot find them at all in the way we naively believe them to exist.

So, not finding what they are and how they actually exist at the most fundamental level is a sign or indication that all things and phenomena are empty of inherent or intrinsic existence. Which means, as we have said over and over again, all things and phenomena do not have any form of self-characterization to exist as what they are. They are not self-enveloped or self-generated to be what they are. They do not have the capability to exist in and of themselves through the force of a self-borne essence. This is verified by modern physics. For example, within a clock there is no findable clock particle which forces a collection of atoms to exist or to be perceived as a clock.

On the other hand, things are capable to function. Things seem to have a capability to affect our experience. Things are able to interact with each other. They are capable of inducing feelings of joy, sorrow, pleasure, pain, and so forth. This can be confirmed through our own experiences. This indicates that things do exist and function. However, we cannot find what they really are at the substantial level when we carefully search for their self-characterized essence. So, the correct way to posit how things actually exist is: They exist only at the level of mere appearance based on characterization given by the conventional mind. Other than that, there is no different or separate way through which things are capable to come into being as what they are. And, the correct way to posit how things function is: They function in accord with our needs.

The question is, can we really be satisfied with things existing only at the level of mere appearance with the capability to function? Unless we come to a conclusion where we are fully satisfied with this, we cannot posit or establish conventional reality or existence. Until we are able to posit the conventional reality, we cannot reconcile the functionality of things and phenomena with their final nature of emptiness, even if we understand intellectually that it is the interdependence of things that allows them to function, to interact with each other.

As we have said repeatedly, when we search for the very existence of the object clock at the fundamental level by going beyond the level of mere appearance, we cannot find anything. We cannot pinpoint or identify anything as a clock at the level of the material base. This indicates that the clock by nature is empty of inherent existence or intrinsic existence. Which means, it is empty of the self-characterization of clock. That object does not have any form of characterization to be a clock without the name clock that is given by an individual subjective mind. At the same time, it can function as a clock. Since it is capable to function to fulfill conventional needs, therefore, it exists. Its functionality is the sign or indication that it is an existent thing, but, at the same time, we cannot find that it really exists at the substantial level. It is not inherently existent.

So, how can we posit that object existing as a clock? Like this— The way this object exists as a clock is only at the level of mere appearance based on the characterization given by the conventional subjective mind. Therefore, unless we are fully satisfied with this object existing as a clock only at the level of mere appearance, there is no way for us to be able to establish or posit its conventional reality. It appears, it has an appearance, but it has no substantial or objective existence. Again, as mentioned earlier, appearance means: One that causes the mind

Critical Point Four: How to Posit Conventional Reality

or consciousness to arise in that aspect or with that content, and this appearance leads the subjective, perceiving mind to name the object.

In general, the way to posit conventional reality is much more subtle than the way to posit emptiness. Therefore, it is extremely difficult to find the complete form of the middle way, the true sense of the middle way.

With this, we have finished the fourth critical point: If things and phenomena are empty of inherent existence, do they really exist? If they exist, how can we posit conventional reality? **Lama Tsongkhapa** said:

> *When we see emptiness in terms of the meaning of dependent origination, then being empty of inherent existence and capable to function do not contradict.*

Things cannot be found at the level of their substantial base, but we cannot deny their existence, because they are capable of inducing for example painful feelings and pleasurable feelings. This indicates that all things—interdependently arisen, impermanent, and having no inherent existence—exist only at the level of mere appearance. Therefore, as we have said, we need to see that, as **Lama Tsongkhapa** said about things in *Lam-tso Nam-sum*, stanza fourteen:

> *Appearance certifies their existence. Emptiness confirms their illusory nature.*

Chapter Twenty

Critical Point Five: Merging Appearance and Emptiness

THE FIFTH AND FINAL critical point in understanding emptiness is how to merge appearance and emptiness with no room for them to be in contradiction, or how to reconcile appearance and emptiness. Recall that the fourth critical point is primarily how to posit conventional reality alongside emptiness. We have established conventional reality under critical point four, and seen at the same time that while they do not have inherent existence, things do exist and function. Now we are looking at how to reconcile appearance and emptiness.

Appearance or *nang-wa*, in Tibetan, certifies the existence of phenomena. Appearance shows us that things and phenomena exist. Emptiness or *tongpa-nyid*, in Tibetan, confirms their illusory nature. Their very nature is illusory. Things appear but we cannot find them under close analysis. They are just like a mirage or a magician's creation, and we cannot find them existing objectively. The mirage appears, but we cannot find whatever we think we see there at an objective level. In the same way, when a magician creates an attractive thing it functions to entertain the conventional mind, but we cannot find it at the material level.

So, *nangwa-tongpa*, in Tibetan, means **appearance cancels the nonexistence of all things and phenomena, and emptiness excludes self-characterization in all things and phenomena.** Therefore, the appearance of an object and its emptiness are complementary and co-inclusive. They are two different perspectives on the same thing. We need to know how to reconcile the appearance which proves the existence of the phenomenon at a conventional level with the unfindability of the phenomenon at the objective level—the absence of intrinsic existence that is called emptiness. We need to reconcile those two as complementary, not contradictory, in order to complete a full realization of emptiness.

Whether or not we can really reconcile those two as complementary primarily depends on how good we are at positing that things and phenomena exist only at the level of mere appearance. We have already discussed this in depth as well as the fourth critical point, how to posit that things existing at the level of mere appearance are fully capable to function. This fifth critical point, how to reconcile and merge emptiness and appearance or functionality, is, like the first four critical points, extremely subtle, somewhat difficult to understand fully.

Reconcile means seeing appearance and emptiness as complementary, not contradictory; deeply related in nature, not unrelated; cohesive, not incohesive. Just because they are deeply related, appearance confirms emptiness and emptiness confirms appearance, rather than emptiness canceling appearance and appearance canceling emptiness.

Identical Relationship

Appearance and emptiness are deeply related in that they have an identical relationship. As we discussed before when talking about impermanence and dependent arising, **identical relationship** between two things means that the two are related and one cannot exist without the existence of the other while these two are part of the same entity. When one goes out of existence, automatically the other goes out of existence. However, the two objects, in this case emptiness and appearance, are not the same, and they are not one. So, therefore, in the *Heart Sutra* we find, "Form is emptiness and emptiness is form. Form is not other than emptiness and emptiness, too, is not other than form." The *Heart Sutra* confirms this identical relationship between emptiness and form by saying that form is emptiness and emptiness is form. Likewise, by implication, it confirms the identical relationship between the appearance of all phenomena and the emptiness of those phenomena.

Since we have already covered at length the meaning of appearance and emptiness, there is no need to again elaborate those two topics. However, we must emphasize that between those two things there is a relationship of identical nature.

Appearance and emptiness are characteristics of every entity, like two sides of the same coin. The two faces of the coin are not the same, but they are in one entity. We cannot say one face is the same as the other, but both faces of the coin are in one entity, the coin. Which means, one face of the coin is inseparable from the other face by nature and vice versa. The two faces of the same coin are in the same entity but are not the same because they have different isolates.

Isolates

An isolate is something that the mind distinguishes as a separate thing. For example, in the case of a coin, the mind isolates a particular thing as **this side** of the coin in relation to **non-this side** of the coin. Similarly, **that side** of the coin is isolated by the mind in relation to **non-that side** of the coin. Therefore, this side of the coin and that side of the coin are established within one entity—the coin. This face is distinguished from that face based on the ability of the mind to isolate those things as two different phenomena although they are of the same nature. In this case they are of the same nature at the same time that they are within one entity. When two things have separate opposing opposites, they cannot be the same thing. Therefore, since this side of the coin and that side of the coin have separate opposing opposites, they are not the same thing. However, they are two different perspectives on the same entity.

Another example: Something being a product and that same thing being impermanent are two different perspectives on the same entity. Those two (product-ness and impermanence) are characteristics of every entity. Even though they are in one entity, these two are not the same because they have different isolates: An object being a product is distinguished by the mind in relation to non-product-ness, and that same object being impermanent is distinguished by the mind in relation to non-impermanent. Product is the isolate of non-product. Impermanence is the isolate of permanence. This shows that product-ness and impermanence are not the same although they are in one entity.

Appearance and Emptiness in One Entity

Earlier we said appearance and emptiness are in one entity with an identical relationship or with the same nature. It is good to keep in mind that appearance and emptiness are in one entity and share the same nature. However, as we have said, this does not mean that they are the same thing. The reason why they are not the same thing even though they are in one entity is because they are different isolates. This is one way to reconcile appearance and emptiness. These two are complementary, not contradictory. They are related, not totally unrelated. These two are cohesive, not incohesive.

Another way to reconcile appearance and emptiness is by showing that dependent origination is not limited to things and phenomena arising from causes and conditions. Similarly, dependent origination is not limited to things arising from parts and fractions. Things are not just coming into being due to the collective work of causes and conditions or due to the collective force of parts and fractions. Rather, dependent origination or dependent arising means that things and phenomena do not have independent status to come into being as what they are. In addition to being reliant on causes and conditions and on parts and fractions they ultimately rely on a subjective designating consciousness, on something other than themselves.

The Full Meaning of Dependent Origination

To reconcile appearance certifying the existence of the phenomena and emptiness confirming the illusory nature of the phenomena, we need to look at the full meaning of dependent origination. **Lama Tsongkhapa** said,

> *One who understands the full meaning of dependent origination, but still does not understand emptiness is really unimaginable.*

The full meaning of dependent origination itself should or must resonate with the fact that all things and phenomena lack the slightest room to be independently existent, inherently existent or intrinsically existent. Similarly, the full meaning of emptiness must directly or explicitly resonate with how things exist interdependently, only through reliance on something other than themselves.

Also, the full meaning of emptiness should not leave room for the possibility that things do not exist. The full meaning of emptiness naturally makes feasible the existence of things and phenomena rather than creating room for the possibility that they do not exist. Emptiness makes their existence feasible, reasonable, conceivable, realistic, rational or imaginable. The full meaning of dependent origination naturally reflects the empty nature of the phenomena. The full meaning of emptiness naturally reflects the interdependent nature of the phenomena. In *400 Verses*, **Aryadeva** said:

Whatever is dependently arisen must not have independent status. Since all things and phenomena are dependently arisen, therefore they must not have intrinsic existence.

Therefore, dependent arising and emptiness are naturally symmetrical, complementary, cohesive and related. Similarly, **Nagarjuna** has said:

Those who understand the emptiness of all things and phenomena, yet also conform to karma and its effects, are more amazing than amazing, more wondrous than wondrous.

This is because emptiness does not affect how the karma forms and functions and never fails to bring its effect. The realization of emptiness makes the law of karma more powerful. Emptiness would seem to make the law of karma less serious, but it really makes it more serious!

Similarly, **Lama Tsongkhapa** has said:

If one sees emptiness strictly in terms of the meaning of dependent origination, then all things being empty of inherent existence and being capable to function do not contradict.

Like that, there are hundreds of quotes from great Tibetan masters like **Lama Tsongkhapa** and his disciples and from great

CRITICAL POINT FIVE: MERGING APPEARANCE AND EMPTINESS

Indian masters from the second century onwards—**Nagarjuna, Chandrakirti, Buddhapalita, Aryadeva, Shantarakshita, Shantideva,** and so on—which keep our minds very busy and entertained. Many monks sit and stroke their beard while their minds are very entertained with comparing the thousands of pages they have memorized. With a minor conscious effort, they can recall different sayings from different masters and then deeply penetrate the meaning of those phrases. It is very relaxing, so there is no occasion for loneliness.

Recapitulation

Now we will recapitulate briefly this fifth critical point, how to reconcile and merge emptiness and appearance. To start: All things and phenomena being dependently arisen by itself makes them empty of inherent existence by nature. The emptiness of all things connotes them as being dependently arisen. Similarly, all things and phenomena being dependently arisen is the unmistakable sign that they are empty of inherent existence by nature, just as being a product—being dependently arisen—is the unmistakable sign that things are impermanent.

So, our understanding of something being dependently arisen brings with it the understanding of that being empty by nature. Similarly, our understanding of something being empty brings with it the understanding of that as being dependently arisen. This is the final way through which we are able to reconcile appearance and emptiness as complementary or as having an identical nature with regard to the same object. Appearance and emptiness are two different tastes of the same thing.

Things and phenomena being dependently arisen makes it impossible to find any primal essence in their material components. Therefore, all things lack any self-generated essence and lack any self-generated characterizations. This is what is meant by emptiness.

Our understanding of emptiness cannot be mature or complete while we still see some kind of conflict between appearance and emptiness. Our realization of emptiness becomes mature and reaches its peak when our understanding of emptiness brings with it appearance and emptiness in perfect harmony. Similarly, our realization of emptiness becomes mature or complete when our understanding of dependent arising brings with it an understanding of emptiness. Those two are mutually supporting and complementary, and they resonate with one another.

Chapter Twenty-one

Summary and Conclusion on the Five Critical Points

WITH THIS, WE HAVE finished our full discussion on emptiness. We have gone carefully through all five critical points:

FIRST, the meaning of dependent origination, and its three dimensions or levels of subtlety, the most subtle being the mode of imputation—how all things rely on a name or term for their existence.

SECOND, the object of negation. To realize emptiness it is first necessary thoroughly to analyze and understand the mode of imputation in order to clearly identify the object of negation—or *gagja*, in Tibetan. The mode of imputation is the way things are imputed or designated by the subjective mind. Once we understand the way things are imputed by our subjective mind to exist as a snake, rope, cup, table, and so forth, then we can realize how we consent to the false appearance of objects as being inherently existent and we can identify the object of negation, the *gagja*.

From studying how to identify the *gagja* we know that it is the intrinsic existence that we wrongly, mistakenly, attribute to all things when we give a name. Objects appear to us as existing by their own power, and we do not take into account that we have subjectively imputed a name upon them. The way things appear to our mind is as if they really exist on their own side, but this contradicts the fact that they exist as such and such only because we name them such and such. If we always have in mind that this object exists as a cup to us because we have imputed the name cup to it, then we can see the discrepancy between the way things are and the way they appear, and that how things actually exist is virtually through imputation and not through their own nature.

Unless we can see the discrepancy between how things appear as if inherently existing and how they really in fact exist, then we cannot identify the object of negation. Once we clearly identify the object of negation, then we can, through the force of our analysis, refute, negate, destroy, defuse or dismantle that wrong appearance and prevent it from arising whenever we see any object. We prevent it from arising by repeating the analysis over and over until we get to the point that at the very moment we see something we know instantaneously that its appearance is deceiving and we no longer have to go through a lengthy process of analysis to refute it. Through the force of analysis during training the second critical point, we fully dismantle wrong appearance and prevent it from appearing on the side of the object.

Regarding the *gagja*, the object of negation, it is important to know that negation does not mean pushing something away. Destroying, dismantling or smashing something through brute force, armed with a tool like a hammer, is not the meaning of negation. Negation means that through the force of the analysis we have prevented that wrong appearance from arising on the side of the object. Whenever we prevent that wrong appearance from arising on the side of the object, then we have ascertained or detected the absence of intrinsic existence. The mere detection of the absence of intrinsic existence through the force of analysis is what we call the realization of emptiness.

The THIRD critical point is just this—the realization of emptiness. At this point the realization of emptiness arises as a mere detection of the absence of the *gagja,* the object of negation. When does the realization of emptiness occur? It occurs the moment you detect the absence of the object of negation. Your detection of the absence of the *gagja* or object of negation comes as the direct result of analysis. The application of analysis is aimed only to detect that absence. Through the force of analysis we come to see that the way things appear to our mind is contradictory to the way things really are. Unless we fully prevent that wrong appearance which never matches the way things really are, we will never detect the absence of inherent existence.

The FOURTH critical point is how to posit the conventional world though all things and phenomena are empty. The conventional world in which we live has things and objects that we see, feel, hear, touch and taste in our everyday life through our five senses. All these objects have their function to fulfill our needs and necessities. However, nothing has intrinsic existence that qualifies such and such object to function in any certain way beyond our need or beyond our choice. This does not mean that things and phenomena do not exist. They do exist but not in the way we ordinarily perceive and think. How do things really exist? Things and objects exist as a mere reference of the conventional name or term that we assign to them so that they can exist for our own use to meet our conventional needs. To repeat—Nothing exists in absolute form. Things exist as a result of mere designation and therefore nothing can be found to be absolute or possessed of rigid characteristics or function.

The FIFTH and final critical point is how to merge appearance and emptiness. You cannot stop at the fourth critical point. You must make effort to reconcile appearance and emptiness, to see that they are complementary, and to see that one cannot exist without the other.

You do this by seeing that any object that appears to your mind is dependently arisen and therefore empty of inherent existence, yet is still able to function, and understanding that any object that is empty of inherent existence is dependently arisen.

All this lengthy discussion on emptiness is summarized, condensed or illustrated in *Madhyamika* logical reasoning by the following logical syllogism:

A table is empty of inherent existence because of being dependently originated.

Table is the subject. Empty is the predicate. Dependently originated is the reason. The natural, identical relationship between the subject, predicate and reason shown in the syllogism explains and leads to three unmistaken final conclusions which prove and establish that all things and phenomena are empty of inherent existence. First, dependently originated must necessarily be present in the subject table and whatever is the subject must necessarily be dependently originated. Second, whatever is dependently originated must necessarily be empty. And third, whatever is inherently existent must necessarily not be empty.

Whatever is dependently originated must necessarily be empty and whatever is inherently existent must necessarily not be empty. These two are a dichotomy—mutually exclusive—and thus one cancels the other. Therefore there cannot be anything that can be both or neither, and there is no third possibility.

Since the subject table is dependently originated, the table must be empty with no possibility for it not to be empty of inherent existence. With this we have finished the discussion on emptiness.

Chapter Twenty-two

Manjushri Practice and Meditation on Emptiness

It is beneficial if you can do Manjushri practice in conjunction with study and meditation on emptiness. In case you as an individual see meaning in doing Manjushri practice to enhance your learning capability through making an intimate connection with Manjushri and using that connection as a channel through which you can receive clarification and blessings from Manjushri, then the instructions for that practice can be found in the following pages.

If you know how to do Manjushri practice with some personal conviction, it can really help. If you do not have some kind of personal belief or conviction in that practice, then there is no certainty that it will help. Simply reciting the Manjushri mantra alone is not sufficient for this practice to be effective. We will give complete instructions for Manjushri practice, but it's up to you whether or not you want to combine this practice with your study on emptiness.

In general, many people do not see the usefulness in these types of practices. This is a big mistake on the part of Western Buddhist practitioners, who seem more interested in dry intellectual information. So, generally, I hesitate to introduce many practices, because I feel most of you will see them as blind faith practices. If you see them as mere faith practices, then they are of no use.

The Manjushri practice, if done with conviction, can be beneficial. I rarely see a balance between study and practice on the part of Western students. Therefore, I think it best to introduce these kinds of practices only for the benefit of those who wish to combine their critical study with real practice.

The best thing is to have a balance between effective practice and critical study. Currently, we are not lacking critical study, but we lack serious practice. So, in case you would like to combine Manjushri practice with your daily study and meditation on emptiness, the instructions for that practice can also be found here. In our effort to gain an actual realization of emptiness and impermanence, it is highly useful and effective to combine that effort with formal meditative practice in relation to Manjushri because the practice of the cultivation of wisdom is very much related to Manjushri.

In general, it is extremely difficult for us to have a clear understanding or realization of emptiness solely as a result of critical study, contemplation and analysis unless we combine that effort with formal meditation practice in relation to Manjushri.

As we said, Manjushri practice is highly useful, helpful and effective to increase the power of intellect or to increase your mental capability in the process of learning, contemplation, meditation and penetration. This is because through Manjushri practice one can receive what we call *jinlab* in Tibetan, which translates as blessing. A blessing is spiritual energy that stimulates your mind. The energetic blessing from Manjushri causes your mind to become: first, sharp, with a power to penetrate beyond the deceptive appearance of all phenomena; second, quick, with more power for learning; third, expansive, capacious or responsive, with more capability to comprehend the subtle reality that is normally beyond the comprehension of our dualistic mind; and fourth, the mind becomes more supple and focused.

Sharpness of mind is the opposite of dullness of mind. Fast and quick in the process of learning is opposite to being very slow in the process of learning. For some, memorizing one sentence takes days and days or weeks and weeks. They memorize something in the morning and by afternoon it is gone. Not only is it gone, but by that same evening it is a complete stranger to them. That is called very slow in learning. Expansiveness or responsiveness of mind is the opposite of having a narrow and rigid mind. Suppleness is the opposite of an unserviceable mind. Focused is the opposite of being scattered and distracted.

The mind has a chronic habit of dissipating its energy in thoughts and emotions. Unless we are able to improve or increase the quality of mind in those four ways, it is extremely difficult for us to have an actual realization of emptiness, no matter how strong our intellectual understanding is. Without increasing the quality of mind in those four ways through Manjushri practice, there is no way for our understanding of emptiness to go beyond a mere intellectual concept. Therefore, it is extremely important to combine our effort for the realization of emptiness with the proper, formal meditation practice relying on Manjushri.

As we said, Manjushri is the Buddha of Wisdom. He is the embodiment of boundless wisdom. Therefore, one could say Manjushri is the source of wisdom. He is the destroyer or eliminator of confusion and misunderstanding, who prevents us from falling into nihilism and absolutism. There are three aspects of Manjushri: White Manjushri, Red Manjushri and Orange Manjushri. Among these three, Orange Manjushri is considered to be the most effective for the development of wisdom and to increase the mind's good qualities in the four ways listed above.

The whole purpose or function of Manjushri practice is to receive energetic stimulation, which causes your mind to gain new qualities, such as being fast, quick, sharp in learning, and supple, focused and quickly responsive to the truth of reality without hesitation, confusion, or misunderstanding.

The Seven Stages of Manjushri Practice

While Manjushri practice has seven stages, the heart of the practice has three main parts:

1. Visualizing of Orange Manjushri.
2. Establishing a spiritual connection or intimacy with Manjushri, that you will maintain during the whole practice and use as a channel to receive stimulation.
3. Reciting the Manjushri mantra.

By correctly engaging in those three, one can receive Manjushri's blessing.

Manjushri practice will be very effective if you can go through seven stages:

1. Taking refuge.
2. Generating love, compassion and *bodhicitta*.
3. Reaffirming your serious interest to study emptiness and to gain realization.
4. Visualizing Orange Manjushri. If possible, visualize Orange Manjushri as inseparable from your guru, the same guru from whom you learned emptiness. If you are not comfortable

visualizing Orange Manjushri as inseparable from your guru, then you can simply visualize Orange Manjushri.

5. Making a heartfelt supplication followed by the recitation of the Manjushri mantra. While you are reciting the mantra, you simultaneously visualize wisdom light or wisdom rays emanating from Manjushri's heart and entering into your heart, causing your mind to become sharp, quick and fast in learning, expansive and responsive to the truth of reality, supple and focused. As a result of the increase in the quality of mind, emptiness—no matter how subtle it is, no matter how it is beyond the grasp of the ordinary dualistic mind—comes within your comprehension. At the same time, that stimulation is helping to eliminate confusion, doubt and misunderstanding about emptiness.
6. Consciously dissolving the visualization.
7. Dedicating your practice, which is the formal way of closing or ending every Buddhist practice.

Your Manjushri practice becomes very effective if you can go through those seven stages in one sitting session. While going through the seven steps, it is best not to have any interference or interruption. Now, here are the detailed instructions for the practice.

Refuge

First, take refuge. In general—and particularly in the Mahayana tradition—every Buddhist practice begins with taking refuge and generating love, compassion and *bodhicitta*. Taking refuge is the active process of reestablishing your spiritual connection with the Buddha, Dharma and Sangha by seeing the Buddha as a flawless, compassionate human guide or teacher who shows us a complete path to Enlightenment from his personal experience, seeing the Dharma—the Buddha's teachings—as the unfailing path to Enlightenment, and seeing the Sangha as outstanding examples from whom we draw inspiration, courage and determination to walk the path to Enlightenment.

The immediate effect of taking refuge is that your mind becomes humble and receptive to the practice that follows. Humility is like the lowland which holds water and all the other conditions for ripening the seeds we are planting. Ego is like the tip of the high mountains where the wind blows all our seeds away. One sign of being highly realized is humility. Being humble is very important. This is what should be occurring in our mind when we take refuge. When we take refuge we are definitely not asking or begging for anything from the Buddha. In the process of taking refuge, we are aspiring to become a Buddha or enlightened one ourselves by following the path given by the Buddha while relying on the Sangha for signs of the effectiveness of that path.

Repeat the refuge formula three times while holding this understanding in your heart and mind:

I go for refuge in the Guru.
I go for refuge in the Buddha,
I go for refuge in the Dharma,
I go for refuge in the Sangha.

Generate Love, Compassion and *Bodhicitta*

The second stage of the practice is to generate love, compassion and *bodhicitta*. This is the active process of connecting ourselves with all sentient beings. It is the active process of connecting our heart with everyone—friends, enemies and strangers—regardless of who they are and how they have treated us in the past, how they treat us now, and how they might treat us in the future. The active process of connecting our heart with everyone by means of generating love involves the sincere and genuine wish for all beings to be happy. If we are really able to let that wish occur in our state of mind, then that is called the generation of love. Similarly, connecting our heart with all sentient beings by generating compassion is the sincere and genuine wish for all beings to be free from suffering and the causes of suffering with a willingness on our part to provide relief from what they are going through according to our means and capability. If we are really able to let that wish occur in our state of mind, then that is called the generation of compassion.

In the process of deliberately cultivating love and compassion, there are three ordinary biased feelings which must be subsided:

1. Attraction to those who help or benefit us in some way.
2. Anger or resentment toward those who hurt or harm us in some way.
3. Indifference towards strangers who are neither helpful nor harmful to us.

These are our normal, very biased attitudes: attraction to loved ones, repulsion to enemies, and total indifference toward strangers. In generating love and compassion, those ordinary biased feelings are subsided and you can build a good healthy attitude toward all beings.

After generating love and compassion, generate *bodhicitta* by means of aspiring to attain Enlightenment, not just for your own sake, but for the ultimate benefit of all sentient beings. In generating *bodhicitta*, you must have a decisive thought, wish or feeling to attain Enlightenment for the sole purpose of benefiting all sentient beings. And it is important to have this thought or wish without doubting your capability. Do not wonder, "Can I or can I not?" or "Am I hoping for a big outcome while I do not have the capability to reach that goal?"

While developing as a student of Buddhism, you will eventually establish with valid logic the capability of all sentient beings to attain Enlightenment. However, while engaging in the daily practice of generating *bodhicitta*, you should not question your capability to attain Enlightenment. Here we are talking about actual practice and not just intellectually defining love, compassion and *bodhicitta*. We are discussing how to effectively strive in developing love and compassion in our hearts and minds through deliberate conscious intent.

At the same time, it is extremely important not to generate love, compassion, and *bodhicitta* and then just immediately forget about these. Rather, allow your mind to remain under the influence of or to remain saturated with genuine feelings of love, compassion and *bodhicitta* throughout the practice. If you let your mind remain saturated with love, compassion and *bodhicitta*, then the possibility of your biased attitudes returning at a later moment during the practice is prevented.

What do we mean when we say "under the influence of"? For example, when a loving mother who has only one loving child loses that child suddenly for some reason, then she goes through great agony, grief and mourning. For days and days, months and months, and maybe years and years, whatever she thinks, whatever she says and whatever she does remain under the influence of those feelings. This is the meaning of "under the influence of."

Influence is not the same as manipulating or forcing your mind in an unintentional direction. If those feelings of love, compassion and *bodhicitta* are not very influential to your behavior in a subsequent moment, then you are generating them in an ineffectual and pretentious way. You should not be pretending that you are loving and compassionate. A new shift in your behavior must occur. When you generate love and compassion, as it says in the text, you should be pregnant with love or pregnant with compassion. That love and compassion become a part of who you are at that moment. It is not a feeling that is separate from who you are.

For example, whenever you are going through the intense emotional feeling of anger, you do not feel that the anger is separate from who you are. When you are going through the intense emotional feeling of anger, at that moment the anger is "you." You cannot separate it from who you are. Similarly, when we have intentionally, deliberately generated the sincere feeling of love or compassion in our mind, that feeling of love or compassion becomes one with us, and there is no way to distinguish that feeling from who you are. This is the experience you should be having. This is called practice.

It is called practice because you are in the active process of internalizing new positive qualities of mind which you have never felt before. Through this, your mind becomes more and more habituated to those new positive qualities of mind. Your mind becomes more and more familiar with those positive qualities as they become part of who you are. As a result you become more and more compassionate, and you are able to spontaneously react with love and compassion in all conditions and circumstances. Then, you have become a compassionate person.

Repeat the following prayer three times while making effort to generate genuine feelings of love and compassion:

> *May all sentient beings have happiness and the causes of happiness.*
> *May all sentient beings be free of suffering and the causes of suffering.*
> *May all sentient beings never be separated from happiness free from suffering.*
> *May all sentient beings abide in equanimity, free from the attachment and aversion which cause them to hold some close and others distant.*

Repeat the following prayer three times while making effort to develop *bodhicitta*, the altruistic wish to seek Enlightenment for the sake of all beings:

> *To the Buddha, Dharma and Sangha, I go for refuge until I am enlightened.*
> *Whatever virtue and merit I create through practicing giving and the other perfections,*

May they serve as an unfailing cause for the attainment of Enlightenment for the sake of all sentient beings.

Re-affirm Your Wisdom Intention

Next, the third step: Re-affirm your serious interest to study and to gain realization of emptiness. You want to make this wish fully active in your heart so it becomes the most persistent, dominant and strong internal driving force to engage in Manjushri practice. This is the one which, in that very moment, drives you to engage in Manjushri practice voluntarily and joyfully.

Visualization of Manjushri

Fourth, visualize Orange Manjushri. Visualization is the process of generating a clear and complete image of Manjushri in the field of your awareness or in the eyes of your mind. This process of visualization involves the deliberate choice or intention to select the clear image of Manjushri as the sole image to appear in your mind so that you may interact with him through recitation of the Manjushri mantra as a means to receive wisdom stimulation.

Once you build the visualized image of Manjushri, you must hold that image in your mind without allowing the mind to become distracted or without allowing the mind to turn away from that image and onto another object. From this point, you must hold the image of Manjushri for the duration of the entire practice period.

If possible, visualize Orange Manjushri as inseparable from your own guru from whom you have received the teachings on emptiness. This means, if you choose to visualize your immediate guru, then—in an ultimate sense—the visualization of your immediate guru is Manjushri, but he appears to your mind in ordinary human form. If you choose to visualize Manjushri, then—in an ultimate sense—the visualization of Manjushri is actually your immediate guru but appearing to your mind as Manjushri.

Also, it is necessary and essential to see and to hold the image of Manjushri as a living, breathing and pulsating being, rather than visualizing him in the form of a statue, thangka painting, computerized image or photograph. If you visualize Manjushri as living and breathing, then it will have a special feedback or special positive impact on your mind.

This is how to build the physical image of Manjushri in your visualization:

1. Imagine the empty nature of all existing phenomena.
2. From that empty nature decide to build Orange Manjushri either on the crown of your head or four feet in front of you at the same height as your eyebrows. Choose one location or the other.
3. In the location you have chosen, conjure or build a fully blooming lotus as a seat or cushion. On that lotus seat visualize the orange seed syllable *Dhi*, the seed syllable of Manjushri. You must visualize the *Dhi* syllable as made of light, with no substantiality on its part.
4. While clearly holding the *Dhi* syllable in that way, imagine that *Dhi* syllable instantly flips into the living, breathing Manjushri described above. Manjushri is seated in the full lotus position. He is wearing pure silk garments which have a rich saffron-like color. His robe is free from wrinkles, dirt and bad odors, and it has the natural quality of repelling the dust of delusive and cognitive obstructions. His right hand holds a double-edged wisdom sword which has a *vajra* hilt and, at the tip, there is a blazing wisdom flame. This sword represents the realization of emptiness that cuts and destroys ignorance, the root of *samsara*. Rather than simply holding this sword, Manjushri is in the active act of cutting ignorance. With the thumb and first finger of

his left hand, he is holding an *upala* stem facing downwards. The stem loops underneath his elbow and rises behind his left shoulder. At the end of this stem, an *upala* flower blooms at the level of his left ear and is the cushion for a *prajnaparamita* text. At the level of ordinary appearance, it is a normal text, but in an ultimate sense, it appears to you as sounds or spoken words which convey the subtle meaning of emptiness, saying:

There is no phenomenon
that is not interdependently arisen.
Therefore, there is no phenomenon
that is not empty of inherent existence.
Form is emptiness;
emptiness is form.
Form is not other than emptiness,
and emptiness, too, is not other than form.

5. Manjushri is adorned with the 112 physical marks of a fully enlightened being. These are listed in my book, *Essential Ethics*, in "Appendix B: Kayas," under "The Thirty-two Major Marks of a Buddha" and "The Eighty Minor Marks of a Buddha." Moreover, he is youthful, attractive, compassionate, energetic, attentive and free of blemishes. Even though you might not be able to visualize all of the 112 physical marks, you should visualize Manjushri with all six characteristics, as youthful, attractive, and so forth. To familiarize yourself with what he really looks like, refer as needed to an image of Manjushri, such as the one on the following page.

6. In your visualization of Manjushri, visualize also the *Dhi* syllable at Manjushri's heart. The *Dhi* syllable is the most prominent, most intense and most radiant syllable of the Manjushri mantra. The remaining six syllables—*Om, Ah, Ra, Pa, Tsa, Na*—are circling or moving around the *Dhi* syllable clockwise, but they are not touching each other.

Manjushri, the embodiment of boundless wisdom.
For a full color image, see digitalthangka.com/my-digital-thangas/

Supplication and Mantra Recitation

Following these six steps of the visualization, which make up the fourth stage of the entire practice, the next major stage is number five, which is to make heartfelt supplication followed by recitation of the Manjushri mantra. Supplication is the sincere and respectful act of invoking the mind of an enlightened being. In this case, we are making an earnest request for Manjushri's compassionate attention:

> *O Guru Manjushri, the source of wisdom and the destroyer of ignorance in the minds of all mother sentient beings, to you I bow and prostrate from my humble and open heart. May I be granted instantaneous wisdom stimulation, so that I can gain a realization of emptiness that is subtle and beyond the comprehension of the ordinary mind.*

After this supplication, simply maintain your visualization and spiritual intimacy with Manjushri that serve as a channel through which you receive wisdom stimulation due to the force of the mindful recitation of the Manjushri mantra. Recite this mantra either 21 or 108 times:

> *Om Ah Ra Pa Tsa Na* **Dhi**

Although each syllable has its own district meaning, here we will give only the general meaning of the complete mantra. The general meaning is:

> *One that ripens the minds of all sentient beings through the force of wisdom stimulation.*

While reciting the wisdom mantra, imagine or visualize wisdom rays radiating from Manjushri's heart and entering into your heart as a result of your mindful recitation. The wisdom rays enter your heart and instantly dispel ignorance, confusion, misconception and misunderstanding in relation to emptiness, causing your mind to become sharp, penetrating, focused, energetic and quick in learning. Through this whole process, emptiness, which is profound and subtle in its very nature, comes within your comprehension.

Dissolution

Next comes the sixth stage, where you dissolve the visualization. First, the mantric syllables *Om Ah Ra Pa Tsa* and *Na* dissolve into the *Dhi* syllable at Manjushri's heart. Second, the wisdom sword dissolves into light and that light dissolves into Manjushri's right side. Third, the *prajnaparamita* text dissolves into light and that light dissolves into Manjushri's left side. Fourth, Manjushri himself dissolves into light and that light dissolves into the *Dhi* at his heart. Finally, the *Dhi* syllable dissolves into light and that light dissolves directly into your heart. Once this occurs, you should deliberately generate a deep sense of joy and bliss.

Dedication

The final and seventh step is dedicating your practice. Dedication is the pure mental act of directing your virtue and merit to becoming the true unfailing cause for transworldly attainments, such as Nirvana and Enlightenment. The most important thing is to have no sense of uneasiness, clinging or grasping onto that virtue and merit for your personal gratification or personal enjoyment, or for your feeling of personal accomplishment. Dedication has three components:

1. The agent or one who dedicates.
2. The virtue and merit that are dedicated.

3. Where or for what your merit is directed—to attain Enlightenment for the sake of all sentient beings.

Dedication is not just an act of spreading out your virtue and merit, throwing them into the air. The dedication of your virtue and merit should have a specific aim. The mental act of just sending out your virtue and merit endlessly or spreading it into the air is not dedication. There are many different dedication prayers, for example:

May all the virtue and merit that I just collected by doing Manjushri practice serve as a cause for attaining Enlightenment for the sake of all sentient beings.

May this virtue and merit that I just created serve to dispel ignorance in the minds of all sentient beings.

May this virtue and merit be the cause for all sentient beings to have a realization of emptiness, the only antidote to ignorance.

You are not simply verbalizing these phrases, saying empty words. The meaning of each phrase is arising in your mental state.

Also, you are not saying, "May all this virtue and merit give me good health. May all this virtue and merit give me good relationships. May all this virtue and merit bring prosperity to my business." Those are not spiritual but merely worldly aims. Some Buddhists who have no formal Dharma education will go to temples and light candles or incense and then recite prayers like those, but those recitations are not proper dedication at all.

Dedication has three functions:

1. Dedication protects your virtue and merit from being destroyed by anger. Anger is the worst enemy of virtue and merit. Therefore, **Shantideva** said:

   One moment of anger can destroy the virtue and merit created over aeons. There is no greater destroyer than anger. There is no greater virtue than patience.

   This morning's virtue and merit can be destroyed by this afternoon's anger. This afternoon's virtue and merit might be destroyed by the late evening's anger. This is a big problem. It is sure and certain that virtue and merit will be destroyed by the force of an instant moment of anger. Therefore, dedication is extremely important to do after every spiritual practice, as well as after performing good deeds. Whenever you do a good deed, even just a few mantra or prostrations, it must be ended with a proper dedication to guard your merit.

2. Dedication prevents your virtue and merit from bringing their results only in your mundane experience.

3. Dedication helps your virtue and merit to keep increasing.

   These are the three functions of dedication.

How to Meditate on Emptiness

With this, we have completed a very concise and brief traditional description of how to do Manjushri practice, and now we'll describe meditation on emptiness, concluding that practice with another dedication. The actual Manjushri practice mainly involves the proper or clear visualization of Manjushri and then recitation of the wisdom mantra while at the same time simultaneously imagining or visualizing the wisdom rays.

Immediately after engaging in the Manjushri practice, it is effective and good to meditate on emptiness. Currently, the more we contemplate the meaning of emptiness, the more our mind becomes dull, numb and lethargic, instead of becoming more sharp, focused, lucid and penetrating. But with the help of wisdom stimulation, your mind is more qualified or more capable to penetrate into the deepest nature of reality—emptiness. Just after the Manjushri practice, while your mind is pretty much calm and peaceful, and more tuned in the way you want, you have a good opportunity to meditate on emptiness.

First, mentally recite this statement of **Nagarjuna** in his *Ratnavali* or *Precious Garland*:

> *The person is not the earth element,*
> *nor the water element,*
> *nor the fire element,*
> *nor the air element,*
> *nor the space element,*
> *nor consciousness.*
> *What else is the person other than those?*

Mentally reciting this statement or stanza while deeply contemplating its meaning can evoke the image of emptiness in your awareness or in your mind's eye. Not finding the person within any of those or outside any of those elements gives you a sense of vacuity or absence of something which you always assumed was findable—an inherent person with the self-characterization of **person-ness**.

Another example, a table:

> *A table is not the top,*
> *nor the bottom,*
> *nor the legs,*
> *nor the shape,*

nor the color,
nor the parts,
nor the whole,
nor any of its material components or constituents.
What else could be found as a table other than those?

Recite this and, while keeping this statement in your mind as clear as possible, begin the analysis to consider if any of the parts of the table could possibly be the table, and similarly, consider whether the whole—the collection of the parts of the table—could be the table, and finally, whether or not the table can be found as separate or other than the parts and whole of the table. After carefully considering in those three ways, you will see that a table cannot be found. The reason why a table cannot be found is because the table lacks inherent existence from its side. The very absence of an inherent self-characterized identity of table—which you always assumed was there—is the true mode of existence of the table and is defined as emptiness. Therefore, as we learned before, emptiness is not mere nonexistence. Rather, it is the ultimate mode of existence for all things and phenomena.

Currently, whenever we see a table, we see that table as existing in and of itself. Not finding the table in any of those three ways indicates the table does not exist intrinsically or at the substantial level. Therefore, logically we should conclude that the table is empty of its own inherent existence. The previous false appearance of the table being intrinsically existent has been prevented or negated through the force of analysis.

Three Points to Be Considered

Through analysis it is not possible to immediately cause the meaning of emptiness to appear in your mind. However, through the force of repeated and effective analysis, the meaning of emptiness is sure to arise in your awareness. There are three points to be considered:

Two Subtle Realities: Impermanence and Emptiness

1. Whatever object you choose as the base for your analysis—a table, cup, chair, house, and so forth—is only used to understand how you normally view things and then to try to find that particular object in the way it normally appears. Normally, things appear to our mind as being inherently solid and substantial. For example, a table appears complete in and of itself as a table. That object appears to our mind as inherently real or substantially existent. We naively assume that the parts, the material components, or the totality—one of those three—has material or substantial characteristics which qualify the object to be what it is. First we have to understand that we think this way. We have to identify that this is how things appear to our mind, that this is how we respond, react and relate to things and objects. This is the basis for our fluctuating emotions, which change beyond our choice.

2. Once we see that this is how we perceive things and this is how they normally appear, then—when we apply the analysis—the ultimate aim of that analysis is simply to find that object in the way it normally appears. Under ultimate analysis, however, we will never find that object in the way it normally appears to our naive, unanalyzing mind. The naive, unanalyzing mind assents to the way things normally appear without the slightest hesitation or second guess. It automatically, spontaneously assents to the way things appear, as if things offer something to grasp onto. It never makes further inquiries, such as, "Do things really exist in the way I see them? Do things really exist in the way they appear?"

As we have already said repeatedly: Through the eyes of the naive, unanalyzing mind, all things and phenomena appear intrinsically real or solidly substantial, which always gives us the automatic impression that the material parts and the totality of the things out there are self-characterized to be what they appear to be. The aim of our analysis is to find the characterizing phenomenon, which causes them to be what they appear to be. We cannot find any characterizing phenomenon. We cannot find this *gagja*, the object of negation. The more we analyze, the less things become findable in the way they appear.

3. Gradually, gradually through the force of repeated analysis, the way things appear to our mind as solidly substantial ceases, melts, dissolves, diffuses or vaporizes. When that very appearance of the object as being inherently solid from its own side dissolves, this is called negation. Therefore, negate does not mean "push it away," "destroy it with a hammer" or "throw it off a cliff." When, through the force of analysis, that which appears to the naive, unanalyzing mind dissolves and no longer appears, that is negation. Once you negate that appearance of inherent existence—the moment it dissolves—what remains in the place of what was negated is a mere vacuity.

The Effect of Meditating on Emptiness

Meditation on emptiness means training our mind to be able to concentrate on that mere vacuity or simply rest in that awareness. Maintaining that experience with sustained effort means being mindful of what you are experiencing. That very manner in which your mind is fully capable to rest in that mere vacuity is actual meditation on emptiness.

The more we do that meditation—the more our mind becomes familiar with that experience of mere vacuity—the less dictating or powerful the appearance of things as being inherently solid will be. The solidity becomes softer or more fragile. All things seem to lack substantiality from their own side and so things seem fragile and incapable to serve as a basis for our assent to their solidity.

Gradually, more and more, things appear to our mind like a water bubble. Once this happens—although we can still have emotions—our emotions are less powerful, less dominant, less controlling, because we realize that they do not have a rooted basis. So they pop up without seeming to be rooted in a justifying outside basis or source. Right now, when we are upset and someone is yelling at us, we constantly see that yelling person as inherently existent and as a justifying reason or cause for our anger or hurt.

As we said before, right now we assume that any of the material components of the table could be the table. We should analyze and analyze until it becomes clear to us that none of the material parts of the table could be the table. We must become very clear about that and fully convinced about that. Next, we must carefully consider whether the totality or the collection of the parts could be the table. Once it becomes clear to us that the collection of parts cannot be the table, then we should consider whether the table could exist separate from its parts and whole. After carefully considering in those three ways, we see clearly that a table cannot be found as the parts or the whole, or separate from all of those. A table cannot be found in any of those three ways. After not finding a table in any of those three ways, our mind will still mull or we will be reluctant to give up on any of those three ways.

We must keep doing this analysis until we become satisfied with not finding the table in any of those three ways, not finding the table in the way it appears. We must keep doing this analysis until the mind is satisfied with the non-findability of the table, and then we become more decisive and comfortable with that experience. At that point, the mind is more qualified to rest in that experience.

Through the process of repeated meditation, your mind becomes familiar with that experience, with the experience of emptiness and, the more your mind becomes familiar with that experience, the less your mind becomes discontent with it. The less the mind becomes discontent with it, the more the mind becomes content with it. This is the process of making yourself acquainted with the reality of emptiness.

Once the table no longer appears to your mind as inherently existent—once that experience of seeing reality happens to you—is there a different way for the table to appear? Before, it could not appear in a new way until we realized that finding the table in the way we expected was impossible and we realized that the true nature of the table is empty of inherent existence. It could not appear in a new way until we realized that not finding the table in the way it appears reveals the true nature of the table or the mode of being of the table. As we meditate on emptiness, the meditation must cause damage to our normal sense of clinging, grasping and attachment to things and objects as if they have substantial reality, as if they exist inherently, while fully confirming their conventional existence. This should happen. If it is not happening to us at all, no matter how much we meditate on emptiness, then this indicates our understanding of emptiness is flawed or not mature.

The Middle Way between Nihilism and Materialism

One last point: It's very important to see the middle way between nihilism and materialism. In general, when we attempt to meditate on emptiness we will struggle between two extremes. When we try to confirm the conventional existence of things and phenomena, we fall into an extreme of either materialism or absolutism. When we look at their conventional existence, we tend to fall into materialism and assume that they exist inherently. When we put more emphasis on their empty nature, then we fall into the extreme of nihilism. If we fall into a nihilistic view, we see all things and phenomena as non-existent. If we see them as non-existent, then they lose their conventional meaning and function. Because the object table, for example, is something that doesn't exist inherently at the material level, we wrongly conclude that it cannot have valid conventional existence at all. Therefore, table disappears or it becomes completely useless and meaningless to us.

So, it is very difficult to avoid the extreme of materialism and the extreme of nihilism and to find the middle path. It is only through repeating time and again the analysis followed by *Shamatha* meditation on emptiness that the Middle Way can be perfected.

With this we have finished the complete instructions for Manjushri practice followed by meditation on emptiness. If you sincerely combine this practice with the study of emptiness, it will make a big difference in your understanding and will help you to gain a flawless realization of emptiness more swiftly.

Afterword

NO MATTER HOW MUCH difficulty we have found in understanding subtle impermanence and emptiness, it is not impossible to gain full realization through our serious effort. We must apply serious effort: first in critical study with a qualified teacher; second, in contemplation and reflection; third, in meditation, which means to become familiar, to gain familiarity; and fourth, in nurturing our understanding of impermanence and emptiness with the wisdom blessings of Manjushri, as well as creating merit through wholesome deeds and enhancing the strength of *bodhicitta* motivation to attain Enlightenment for the universal benefit.

The two subtle realities, impermanence and emptiness, are presented together in one book because within the nature of every object are those two subtleties that are not obvious to our ordinary perception. Subtle impermanence is the first of these two, but as we have learned it is not the final nature of the object. Emptiness of inherent existence is the final nature of the object, the ultimate mode of being of all things and phenomena.

About the Author

Geshe-la obviously has all the Buddhist knowledge and personal experience, and he reflects that with his calmness but also with an incredible sense of humor. He uses his amazing vocabulary to express complex concepts according to everyone's individual mental activity. ~ Charleston Magazine

GESHE DAKPA TOPGYAL, a Tibetan Buddhist monk, was born in the Western region of Tibet, and fled to India at the age of six with his family due to the Chinese invasion of Tibet. He entered Drepung Loseling Monastery at the age of ten and received his Geshe degree (Doctorate of Religion and Philosophy) twenty-two years later in 1992.

Before coming to the United States, he taught in Europe for a number of years. Between 1993 and 1994, he visited one hundred and twenty American cities giving lectures on Tibetan Buddhism and culture, and led a number of meditation retreats. Currently, he teaches students year round and serves as spiritual director of the Charleston Tibetan Society Dharma Center as well as the South Carolina Dharma Group in Columbia, South Carolina. In addition to the book list in this text, Geshe Topgyal has published numerous practice manuals.

www.ingramcontent.com/pod-product-compliance
Lightning Source LLC
Chambersburg PA
CBHW030149100526
44592CB00009B/191